CW00473059

Language and the Nation

The Language Question in Sub-Saharan Africa

AYỌ BAMGBOṢE

EDINBURGH UNIVERSITY PRESS

for the International African Institute

© Ayọ Bamgboṣe, 1991

Edinburgh University Press
22 George Square, Edinburgh

Typeset in Alphacomp Century
by Pioneer Associates Ltd, Perthshire, and
printed in Great Britain by
Redwood Press Ltd, Melksham, Wiltshire

British Library Cataloguing
  in Publication Data
Bamgboṣe, Ayọ
  Language and the nation:
  The question of language in
  sub-Saharan Africa.
  I. Title
  306.40966

ISBN 0 7486 0306 9

Contents

Tables

Preface

This book arises from several years of involvement in the theoretical and practical problems of language development in Sub-Saharan Africa. In spite of the enlightenment on language problems in the region brought about by the volume *Language Problems of Developing Nations* (Fishman *et al.* 1968), and the well-publicized Language Survey of Eastern Africa, 1965–1973, sponsored by the Ford Foundation, there is still considerable ignorance (judging by the questions frequently asked) about the nature and scope of the language question in the region. This book, therefore, focuses on the problems of multilingualism in relation to national integration, communication, development and education. It examines closely the processes of policy formulation and discusses different types of language policies and practices in the context of the role of national and international agencies of language planning. Although the focus of the book is Sub-Saharan Africa, comparisons with other regions of the world are brought in where necessary.

I wish to acknowledge the opportunities I have had for involvement in language problems through association with Unesco, the Ford Foundation, the West African Linguistic Society, the Language Association of Eastern Africa, the National Language Centre (Lagos), and the Nigeria Educational Research Council.

The writing of this book has been made possible by the assistance of a number of institutions: the University of Ibadan, from which I was on sabbatical in the academic year 1987–8; Clare Hall, University of Cambridge and the British Council, which provided fellowships for the period; and the University of Pennsylvania, to which I made an exchange visit in March and April of 1989.

Ayọ Bamgboṣe
Ibadan

Introduction

A language question arises whenever there are language problems requiring a solution. In this sense, there is hardly any country in the world in which there is no language question. If a country is monolingual, there may be the problem of regional or social dialects, or alternatively, the influx of immigrants may bring in minority languages in respect of which action will be required, at least in education. On the other hand, if a country is multilingual, the problems are more pronounced, as action will be required not only in education but in language policy as it relates to communication and administration as well.

The language question in Sub-Saharan Africa arises from the fact that not only are most of the countries multilingual, the colonial experience has led to the importation of foreign official languages which have taken on the roles of national communication, administration and medium of education from early or late primary to university level. Thus, the existing multilingual situation is compounded by the addition of imported languages whose strength does not lie in numbers of speakers, but rather in the superior roles assigned to them. Since the imported official languages are spread through the educational process and education was (and in several countries still is) largely restricted to a few, the population came to be divided into an elite that could speak the official language and the masses that were either illiterate or literate only in an indigenous language. The crux of the language problem in Africa has, therefore, been the pursuit of solutions to language choice in different spheres. For example, in education, to ensure that as many children as possible are given a meaningful education and that illiteracy is eradicated among both children and adults; and in communication and administration, to ensure that participation in local and national affairs is not restricted to the few who can use the official languages but is organized in such a way as to make mass participation possible.

It should be clear from the above that the language question in Sub-Saharan Africa has its origins in two main factors: multilingualism and the colonial legacy. But two other factors have since arisen, namely, the complexities of the demands on a modern state, and the attitudes of governments.

Apart from a handful of countries (all told, fewer than ten), Africa south of the Sahara is multilingual. The incidence of multilingualism may be measured by comparing size of population with number of languages. Countries with large populations understandably also have a large number of languages. For example, Kenya has a population of 20.6 million (and has 35 languages), Sudan 21.55 million (133 languages), Tanzania 22.49 million (113 languages), Zaire 29.93 million (206 languages), Ethiopia 43.35 million (92 languages) and Nigeria 95.19 million (400 languages). But even countries with small populations also have many languages. For example, Cameroon has a population of 9.87 million (and 183 languages), Ghana 13.5 million (57 languages), Côte d'Ivoire 9.81 million (58 languages), Congo 1.74 million (31 languages) and Angola 8.75 million (29 languages).[1]

Multilingualism is often associated with a number of problems. There is the problem of communication. How will the nation function unless there are one or more languages that can be used for national communication and administration? If a choice has to be made, what should be the relevant criteria to be used in making the choice? There is the problem of education. Which of the many languages are to be used as media of instruction and which should be taught only as subjects? Again, if a choice has to be made, what should be the basis for recognition of the 'approved languages'? If several languages are selected for use in education, what will be the cost of the language development work that will be entailed, particularly as set against other priorities on which resources could have been put?

Because of the problems associated with it, multilingualism is often seen as a liability, and the popular attitude is to associate it with 'the curse of Babel'. But multilingualism is not without its positive aspects. Since a language is an embodiment of a culture, the existence of several languages means the cultural enrichment of a country. If there is variety in the fauna or flora of a country, this is seen as a positive aspect of nature; and environmentalists are keen to urge the preservation of the species. But curiously enough, variety in languages does not seem to be welcomed in the same way. Shouldn't the cultural enrichment associated with multiplicity of languages also be seen as a positive endowment by nature? Another positive advantage of multilingualism is that it leads to an incidence of individual bilingualism. Since people have to communicate across language barriers, it follows that some people will have to acquire a language other than their own. In this way, the bilingual person becomes an asset to the community, particularly if, in the process of becoming bilingual, he or she becomes bicultural as well. Indeed, in the African situation, a person who speaks several languages is to be regarded as a better integrated citizen than one who is only proficient in one language, even if that language happens to be the country's official language.[2]

A census of the number of languages spoken in a country often plays down the incidence of bilingualism. The fact is that speakers of smaller languages tend to learn bigger ones, particularly if the languages happen to be close to one another geographically. Hence, there are not only shared languages, but the languages can be differentiated into major ones that have millions of speakers and minority ones. Besides, many of the languages in a given region may belong to the same language family, and this sometimes means that they share certain typological characteristics.

Multilingualism certainly poses a problem for language policy. But it is not an insuperable problem. In fact, a major challenge for those who have to formulate policy is coping with the problem while at the same time harnessing the positive advantages of the phenomenon of multilingualism.

The imposition of colonial rule on dependent territories obviously meant the imposition of a language of administration. The language of central administration was the metropolitan language, but some African languages were used in local administration, for example, in the so-called native courts. The language of education varied according to the perception by the colonial powers of their ultimate goals. The French and the Portuguese, with their declared policy of assimilation, encouraged their own languages and discouraged African languages. The British and the Belgians, on the other hand, favoured a policy of separate development for their colonial subjects and so allowed the teaching of African languages.[3] The Germans favoured a German medium in the schools in their territories, except in East Africa where Swahili was already spreading as a lingua franca.[4]

Colonial educational policies led to the conscious breeding of an elite. Macaulay's justification in India for this policy was as follows:

> It is impossible for us with our limited means to attempt to educate the body of the people. We must at present do our best to form a class who may be interpreters between us and the millions we govern – a class of persons Indian in blood and colour, but English in tastes, in opinions, in morals and in intellect. To that class we may leave it to refine the vernacular dialects of the country, to enrich those dialects with terms of science borrowed from the Western nomenclature, and to render them by degrees fit vehicles for conveying knowledge to the great mass of the population.[5]

The education envisaged was an elitist one: English for the few who would later train the many in their indigenous languages. This, of course, presupposes that the few will also be proficient in their own languages. The major twist to this policy in India and elsewhere was that the few succeeded in English largely to the detriment of their own languages; and, rather than being able to train the masses, they became alienated from them. As a Government Commission in India observed, 'Use of English as such divided the people into two nations, the few who govern, and the many who are governed, the one unable to talk the language of the other and mutually uncomprehending.'[6]

The divergent language policies pursued by the colonial powers led to the entrenchment of different systems of education with emphasis on different types of languages as media of education. Coupled with this was the creation of artificial borders, as a result of the partitioning of Africa by the different powers, in which identical linguistic groups were separated and subjected to the use of different official languages. Two major effects of these policies are the difficulty of co-operation between countries with similar peoples and interests, and the linguistic barrier created which impedes communication between countries in the same region. These problems have persisted even after the countries concerned have become independent. This is mainly because the patterns already established have proved so strong that departure from them has been extremely difficult; and this difficulty is further compounded by the continuing ties with the former colonial powers. For example, former French colonies look mainly to France for trade ties, technical assistance, specialist training, monetary standard, and external tele-communications; and the same is largely true for the others: former British, Portuguese and Spanish colonies having their main external ties with Britain, Portugal, and Spain respectively. It is not unusual, for instance, for cables between two contiguous West African countries to be routed through Paris and London. A constant preoccupation in Africa is the deploring of this division and periodic calls for the situation to be rectified.

The colonial legacy is a recurrent factor in the language policies of African governments. In practically all fields (education, communication, administration, politics and develop-ment), the question has always been whether or not it is desirable or even possible to break away from the existing practices, and if so at what cost. This constant pull between retention and change constitutes the major point of departure as well as a dilemma for language policy-makers.

A modern state requires for its proper functioning high-level manpower, technology and contacts with the outside world. The complexities of these demands impose a constraint on the language policies of African nations. Whatever they do with their indigenous languages, they will need a major world language for access to higher education, science and technology; and this same language will serve as their window on the outside world. In this connection, the colonial legacy proves to be an advantage in that such a language already exists in the imported official language. The question that remains to be settled is the scope that it should have in relation to the indigenous languages. Should these requirements dictate a policy that aims to make everyone function in the imported official language or should varying degrees of participation be recognized involving the exploitation of the indigenous languages for certain functions and the imported official language for others? For example, is it not possible for low-level technology to be domesticated and transmitted in local languages for cottage industries, while high-level technology remains the preserve of the imported official language?

The attitudes of African governments to language problems constitute another factor in the language question. Confronted with the colonial legacy and the difficulty of making a change, they may simply accept the situation as a *fait accompli* or they may remain indifferent. Sometimes, they are aware that there is a problem, but they are so overwhelmed by the magnitude of the problem that they stick to what already exists. It is only in a minority of cases that there have been brave attempts to face the problems squarely and take decisive policy measures; but, even in such cases, the legacy of the past often limits what can be done.

There is a general feeling that language problems are not urgent and hence solutions to them can wait. It is true that the effects of not taking action on a language question may not show up in the same way as those of not taking action on an economic problem (which could show up in terms of inflation, unemployment, fall in production, debt accumulation, etc.). But the fact that the effects are hidden does not make them less serious or mean that they will somehow disappear. A Commission that reported on the Public Service in Nigeria found that the language problem which the Government had been neglecting had serious implications for the performance of workers and therefore for effective administration:

> An overriding problem, which affects the public service as it does all aspects of society is that of language. Nigeria shares with many developing, and some developed countries, the lack of an indigenous *lingua franca*. What this means for efficiency in the conduct of government business is rarely even thought about perhaps because there seems to be no immediate answer. But it is perfectly clear to the careful observer that below the top-most levels in the various sectors of society most people are conducting their business in a language which, in varying degrees, they have not in fact mastered.[7]

Not only is avoidance of the language problem unjustified, the (analogous) attitude of making pronouncements that cannot be implemented is also a form of avoidance. The longer a solution to a language problem is delayed, the more difficult it will be eventually to solve it.

In the chapters that follow, the language question is examined in relation to national integration, national development, communication and education.

In their search for national integration, African countries, like many newly independent nations, look for symbols that could reinforce the sentiments of oneness. Language is one such symbol. But since language is often associated with ethnicity, fostering national integration is usually seen as de-emphasizing multiplicity of languages, just as building a nation is seen as synonymous with breaking down ethnic loyalties. The association of multilingualism with divisiveness is unjustified, since language is only a convenient scapegoat on which the real causes of divisiveness are usually hung. A national language can be a powerful symbol and rallying point for nationalism, but it does not follow that a national feeling cannot be developed in the absence of such a language. In the world today, the one-language nation state is the exception rather than the rule. For most African nations, the road to national integration can only be through more than one language. Each language will have defined roles, and if a single national language eventually emerges, it can only be as a result of a gradual process involving a transitional period of planned bilingualism.

National development is often defined narrowly in socio-economic terms. But even within such a restricted definition, the role of language is important. This can be shown in the link between literacy and development. The world's poorest countries are also the countries with the highest rates of illiteracy. Since literacy liberates untapped human potential and leads to increased productivity and better living conditions, it is not surprising that countries with the highest rates of literacy are also the most economically advanced. Similarly, mass communication with its emphasis on flow of information can provide a suitable climate for national development. But it is even mistaken to equate national development with socio-economic development. A wider and more satisfactory conception of national development is that it is concerned with total human development. In this sense, education in general and mass participation in the economic process are vital to development; and the only way to ensure mass involvement is to pay more attention to the use of indigenous languages in education (especially in adult literacy) and the mass media. Given Africa's high illiteracy rates, there does not seem to be any other viable alternative.

Communication is essential to the proper functioning of a nation state. Such communication may be at the local, regional or national level. There is also the need for communication between nation states. Given the high degree of multilingualism in Africa, an appropriate model of communication must envisage different types of languages in different roles. This also presupposes some degree of bilingualism for the citizens of most countries. The pattern of communication may differ from country to country, but the essential ingredients of hierarchical roles for languages and bilingualism are likely to be constant. Although there are African languages spoken across national boundaries, the existing pattern of international communication, which is through the former colonial languages, is likely to persist for the reason that there are no viable alternatives for the moment nor are there likely to be in the foreseeable future.

Language education may involve the use of a language as a medium of instruction or simply for initial literacy or its teaching as a subject. Which language is selected for which purpose and at which level of education are all options that, in theory, educational authorities are free to decide upon. In practice, however, there are constraints, which may be historical, economic, socio-cultural, pedagogic or political, which limit the freedom of choice. In particular, the colonial legacy seems to determine current educational practices as it has proved virtually impossible in all but a few cases to break away from the inherited practices. The main point of contention is usually the role of mother tongue education in relation to education in an imported official language. The latter has been the major medium of education even from the primary level. The need for secondary and higher education which for most countries can only be given in this language tends to favour the continuation of the practice. But negative results from it show that there is perhaps a need to try out alternatives. This has led to experimentation in the use of African languages as media of instruction in primary education. Even when positive results have been forthcoming from the experiments, such is the strong hold of the past that change in the direction of the positive findings has been resisted or slow in coming. The challenge in language education is not only to ensure a meaningful mother tongue education, but also to evolve a viable programme in which both mother tongue and other tongue teaching reinforce each other.

The various areas in which the language question arises call for a co-ordinated plan of solutions. This must involve the formulation of policies and the provision of mechanisms for their implementation. Models of language planning provide a paradigm as to how this should be done. However, African language policies are generally characterized by avoidance, vagueness, arbitrariness, fluctuation and declaration without implementation. Besides, a great many language activities are undertaken by private agencies with or without government approval. A strict application of some models to these practices will probably exclude them from the scope of language planning. While it will be desirable for decisions to take account of a variety of inputs which may be supplied by experts, there is also a need for language planning models to be more flexible so as to be able to embrace different modes of decision-making as well as different language improvement practices, whether or not they are carried out by government agencies.

Notes to Introduction

1. The population figures are taken from Unesco (1987), while the number of languages spoken in each country is from Grimes (1974).
2. See Kashoki (1982: 24).
3. See Spencer (1971).
4. See Mehnert (1973).
5. Quoted in Dakin (1968: 6–7).
6. Quoted in Duggal (1981: 50).
7. See Federal Republic of Nigeria (1974: 4, para 17).

1

Language and National Integration

The Integrative Process

One of the legacies of colonial rule in Africa is the creation of many artificial states in which several ethnic groups have been brought together under one administration within a single territory. A major preoccupation of many African countries is, therefore, how to ensure the continued 'oneness' of their states as well as the forging of a bond of belonging together as nationals of the state. National integration, as this preoccupation is generally known, may be defined as essentially consisting of 'creating or strengthening within the borders of a country a collective sentiment of belonging together irrespective of individual or subgroup differences' (Alexandre, 1968).

It is generally accepted that one way of ensuring integration is to bring the groups together in interaction and conflict, with the result that a basis is found for compromise and working together for the development and progress of the country.[1] This is already happening in many countries where economic, political and educational arrangements have to take into consideration the pluralistic nature of the society, including the incidence of uneven development.

National integration is often fostered through a series of overt measures designed to reinforce the sentiment of oneness.[2] Such measures include power-sharing through zoning of political and bureaucratic posts, a legal requirement for a multi-ethnic base for political parties, special programmes designed to bring young people together (such as Ghana's Young Pioneers, Nigeria's National Youth Service Corps and similar programmes in Tanzania and Zaire) and ideologies designed to raise national consciousness (such as Kenyatta's Harambe in Kenya, Nyerere's Ujamaa in Tanzania, Kaunda's Humanism in Zambia, Banda's four cornerstones of Unity, Loyalty, Discipline and Obedience in Malawi and Nigeria's Military Government's War Against Indiscipline/Mass Mobilization for Social and Economic

Reconstruction). There are, of course, more obvious national symbols such as the national flag, the national anthem, the national day, the national football team, and several national monuments, all of which are designed to provide a focus of national identity.

Language and Ethnicity

Perhaps the most important symbol often invoked in connection with national integration is a national language. This is a natural step, since language is often associated with ethnicity, and the latter is assumed to be an impediment to national integration. But how valid is it to equate language with ethnicity? If the equation is valid, one would not expect any member of an ethnic group to speak more than one language nor members of different ethnic groups to speak the same language. The fact is that both situations occur quite frequently.[3] Swahili is spoken as a second language by different ethnic groups in Eastern and Central Africa just as Hausa is spoken by different ethnic groups in West Africa. The reverse is also true in that different languages may be spoken by a single ethnic group. This may be taken in the sense of members of an ethnic group regularly learning another language, as when the Iṣẹkiri learn and use Yoruba as their second language or in the sense of an ethnic group speaking different but historically related languages, for example the Ẹdo ethnic group in Nigeria, which speaks several languages belonging to the Edoid group of languages.

It is clear, then, that merely equating language with ethnicity is a fairly weak position. It would appear that there are four plausible positions in this matter, each recognizing the existence of other factors in addition to language:

1. *Language is crucial by itself.* According to this position, language is one of the factors that determine ethnicity, but there is no other factor 'as powerful as language in maintaining by *itself* the genuine and lasting distinctiveness of an ethnic group' (Giles and Saint-Jacques 1979: ix). Although this position is a popular one, it can easily be faulted because there are ethnic groups which have virtually lost their language and yet continue to feel a sense of being distinctive -- for example, the Fulani in Northern Nigeria who have virtually given up their language, Fulfulde, for Hausa and yet continue to see themselves as ethnically distinct. A similar case is that of

the Scots, who no longer speak Gaelic but English, and yet maintain their ethnic identity. Clearly, there must be some other factor at work that gives rise to such a feeling of distinctiveness.

2. *Language is not crucial at all.* According to this position, ethnicity merely reflects an 'us versus them' feeling, and language and other seemingly identity-marking features may be discarded without affecting it. In fact, the crucial thing is self-identification and self-awareness of being different. According to Connor (1972: 337), scholars tend rather 'to perceive ethnic nationalism in terms of its overt manifestations than in terms of its essence. The essence of a nation is not tangible. It is psychological, a matter of attitude than of fact.' Although there is much to be said for this viewpoint, it has one serious drawback. It plays down the significance of language which, like other manifestations, is believed to be a minor element and merely a convenient peg on which to hang a deep-seated feeling which is more abstract. While it is true that a language can be discarded, its evocation and use *as a symbol* continue to be very important. The example of the Fulani given above demonstrates this very clearly. For them, the language remains a powerful symbol.

3. *Language is only important in relation to other factors.* Language is one of the complex of factors and cultural elements that determine ethnicity; however, what is important is not language difference or identity as such, but the presence as well of other identity-marking factors. As Deutsch (1953: 71) puts it, 'What counts is not the presence or absence of a single factor, but merely the presence of sufficient communication facilities to produce the overall result. The Swiss may speak four different languages and still act as one people, for each of them has enough learned habits, preferences, symbols, memories, patterns of landholding, all of which together permit him to communicate more effectively with other Swiss than with speakers of his own language who belong to other peoples.' One could even go on further to say that the perception of these factors and judgement about them is more important still.

This position is valid in that it does not propose a one-to-one correspondence between language and ethnicity, and, at the same time, it recognises the importance of language in relation to other factors.[4] In this sense, it is compatible with the symbolic function of language in ethnic identity.

4. *Language has a variable role.* According to Ross (1979), the relationship between language and ethnicity varies according to the stage of the grouping involved. Ethnic identity is only one form of collective identity, and each ethnic identity carries with it a different role for language. For example, a communal group is bound together by its language, a minority group is defined by reference to a larger group which dictates the role and scope of its language, while an ethnic group effectively and consciously employs language as a symbol of ethnic mobilization.

Although the postulated progression from communal through minority and ethnic stages to a national stage appears to be an idealization, the emphasis on the functional and symbolic role of language in relation to ethnicity is entirely justified.

Discussions of ethnicity and language should focus not so much on the direct relationship between the two, but rather on the potential uses and abuses of language in promoting ethnicity. It is not language by itself that matters, but the symbolism attached to it. It is this that can be invoked in impeding or furthering national integration.

A favourite paradigm for the discussion of integration is the tribe-to-nation approach. An opposition is presented between the tribe and the nation.[5] The tribe is said to be characterized by ethnic loyalty, a reluctance or resistance to accept national authority, and persistent conflict with rival groups. The nation, on the other hand, is cohesive, politically organized with broad support and legitimacy, and regarded as crucial to fostering national identity and development. This opposition as well as the analogous one between tribalism and nationalism is a gross distortion in the sense that the characteristics associated with tribalism in terms of common attachment to one's own group in preference to an outside group are really not different in kind from those associated with nationalism. As Gellar (1973: 409) has rightly remarked:

> What is called tribalism in Africa is part of the universal
> and timeless problem of how culturally pluralistic
> societies hold together and function within the framework
> of a single political system.

The tribe-to-nation approach to integration can also be, and has

been, faulted on the grounds that it falsifies the history of
original African empires (e.g. Songhai, Mali, Hausa–Fulani,
Ghana, Benin, etc.) which had existed long before the colonial
period, since tribes and tribalism are more appropriately
creations of the colonial era rather than a survival from the pre-
colonial period.[6]

Notwithstanding the above, the colonial legacy has left Africa
with many artificial nations in which several ethnic groups
have been brought together under one administration within a
single territory. Not only do these groups see themselves as
distinct sociocultural entities (e.g. Hausa, Igbo, Yoruba in
Nigeria; Akan, Ga, Ewe in Ghana; Shona, Ndebele in
Zimbabwe; Bemba, Nyanja in Zambia, etc.), there are even sub-
ethnic groups that previously saw themselves as distinct. For
example, when Koelle was collecting word-lists in Sierra Leone
in the 1840s, the people now known as the Yoruba identified
themselves by the dialectal variants Ọyọ, Ẹgba, Ijẹbu, Ijẹsa,
etc., and resented being called Yoruba, a term which they
associated with the Ọyọ.

Language standardization has been a factor in bringing about
a consciousness of being one. Hence, the development of a
written standard for Yoruba which served as a koine for the
different dialectal groups, the emergence of Shona from a
variety of dialects, and the recognition of the linguistic unity of
the various dialects of Akan have, in some way, reinforced the
sentiment of group identity.

Multilingualism and National Integration

Arising from the false association of language with ethnicity,
two complementary myths have developed around the concept
of language and the nation. The first is that multilingualism is
a barrier to national integration; the second is that national
integration necessarily involves the emergence of a nation state
with *one* common language.

The myth that multilingualism impedes national integration
is a widespread one. It is expressed in such views as the
following:

> . . . differences between indigenous languages keep the
> people apart, perpetuate ethnic hostilities, weaken
> national loyalties and increase the danger of separatist
> sentiment. (Schwarz 1965: 39)

Each local language is, moreover, intimately related to a tribal culture; thus use of a local language reinforces attachment to a tribe, thereby going against the current of national sentiment, which is only slightly developed. (Alexandre 1972: 88)

As has been pointed out earlier, it is not language that divides but the attitude of the speakers and the sentiments and symbolism attached to the language. As Fishman (1968a: 45) has rightly pointed out,

differences do not need to be divisive. *Divisiveness is an ideologized position* and it can magnify minor differences; indeed it can manufacture differences in language as in other matters almost as easily as it can capitalize on more obvious differences. Similarly, *unification is also an ideologized position* and it can minimize seemingly major differences or ignore them entirely . . .

An example of differences being played down can be seen in the way some lingua francas are emerging in Africa. Because of the utility of such languages as Akan in Ghana, Wolof in Senegal, Hausa in Northern Nigeria, Lingala in Zaire, not to mention the more widely-spoken Swahili in Eastern Africa, speakers of different languages are embracing them as second languages. Another example is the way differences in dialects which have been magnified in the past almost to the point of language status are now played down considerably (e.g. Twi and Fante,[7] which are now seen simply as dialects of Akan). The converse of this is that differences between closely-related languages which have largely been ignored in the past may suddenly assume a major dimension. For example, the Efik--Ibibio dialect cluster in Nigeria has for years been accepted as practically one language, with Efik as the literary form of the language. This position is now being reversed and Ibibio is more and more being emphasized as a separate language with its own orthography. This trend is likely to be intensified with the creation of a new state, Akwa--Ibom, in 1987 in which the Ibibio form the dominant group.

Some of the real causes of divisiveness in African countries have nothing to do with language. They include exploitation of ethnicity by the elites in order to gain political or economic advantage, the problem of sharing scarce resources with the inevitable competition (e.g. for jobs, positions, facilities, etc.), uneven development, and sometimes external instigation based on nationalistic, ideological or religious motives.

Arising from a distrust of multilingualism, it is often believed that the most suitable model for national integration is through a single common language. As Isayev (1977: 192) puts it, 'Language is a nation's most obvious and most important attribute. There is no such thing as a nation without a common linguistic basis.' Some of the advantages claimed for the model are that it strengthens national unity, it makes planning easier, as there will not be any unnecessary duplication of effort (for example, there will be common educational facilities), there will be no communication gap between the elites and the masses, and maximum participation by all citizens in the system is assured. In spite of these advantages, it is also recognized that unless there are already unity-inducing factors in the country, the deliberate use of language as an instrument for forging national unity in a multilingual country may lead to conflict and disunity.[8] The well-known examples of Hindi in India and Sinhalese in Sri Lanka where attempts to unify through a common language have led to riots are reminders of what could happen in any multilingual situation.

The one-language nation state is a nineteenth-century concept of nationhood which is of little relevance in the world today. As Kelman (1971: 34) has rightly pointed out, 'it goes without saying that a common language is not a necessary condition for a unified state and that one or more major language groups can coexist with minimal conflict between them'. In any case, even a single-language nation may mask serious social, economic or religious divisions within the country, as well as the problem of minority groups who have to become bilingual or else make use of the services of those who are bilingual in the official language and their own language or languages.

If the requirement that a country should have one language spoken by an overwhelming majority of its people were to be applied to Africa south of the Sahara, and a cut-off point of 90% of the population in each country were allowed in defining the monolingual requirement, fewer than ten countries would qualify. They are:

> Burundi (language: Kirundi) 99%, Lesotho (Sotho) 99%, Somalia (Somali) 98%, Madagascar (Malagasy) 98%, Botswana (Tswana) 97%, Seychelles (Creole) 93%, Rwanda

(Kinyarwanda) 95%, Mauritius (Creole) 94%, Swaziland (Swati) 91%. Of these languages, two pairs, Kirundi, Kinyarwanda and Tswana, Sotho, are closely related.[9]
The other countries divide into three groups:

1. *Countries with a predominant language, but spoken by less than 90% of the population.* Tanzania (Swahili), Mali (Bambara), Senegal (Wolof), Ghana (Akan), Central African Republic (Sango), Niger (Hausa), Togo (Ewe), Zimbabwe (Shona), Malawi (Chichewa), Gambia (Wolof), Equatorial Guinea (Fang), Mauritania (Arabic), Burkina Faso (Moore).

2. *Countries with more than one dominant language.* For example: Nigeria (Hausa, Igbo, Yoruba), Zaire (Lingala, Kikongo), Zambia (Bemba, Nyanja, Tonga), Sudan (Arabic, Dinka), Kenya (Swahili, Kikuyu, Luo), Ethiopia (Amharic, Oromo, Tigrinya), Angola (Umbundu, Kibundu, Kikongo), Guinea (Fulfulde, Malinke, Susu), Guinea-Bissau (Balanta, Fulfulde).

3. *Countries with several non-dominant languages.* For example: Cameroon (Douala, Pidgin, Bulu, Gbaya, Fulfulde), Côte d'Ivoire (Anyi-Baule, Dyula, Senufo), Sierra Leone (Krio, Mende, Temne, Kpele), Liberia (Kpele, Grebo, Kru, Vai), Benin (Fon, Gun, Adja, Yoruba, Bariba).

It should be obvious from the above grouping of countries that a monolingual model of integration is out of the question for most African countries. It is feasible for those countries that are almost unilingual and perhaps for those in which there is a predominant language; but, as we shall see, few of these countries have taken advantage of the situation to promote an African language as an instrument of integration. This is because of the hold on most countries of the erstwhile colonial language which in most cases continues to be the sole official language.

With those countries that have several dominant or non-dominant languages, integration can only be seen in terms of several languages coexisting within the state or nation. A multilingual model of integration will, of course, entail serious efforts at language planning and perhaps some considerable costs in operating the administrative and educational system in more than one language. Particular problems will arise in the case of those countries that have several non-dominant languages. In some of them (for example, Sierra Leone), a non-dominant language which is becoming a second language for many may be elevated to the status of an official language; in others (such as Benin), closely related languages may be subsumed under a common language and so attain the status of a majority language.[10] One thing, however, is clear. Even in those countries where a major language can become the official language, provision will have to be made for meaningful roles for the other languages, for example, in primary education.

There is no reason to suggest that a multilingual model will impede integration. In fact, its major strength could be its flexibility and the scope it allows for greater participation by different linguistic groups. In any case, as Das Gupta (1968: 24) has rightly pointed out, national integration 'cannot be built by denying or deriding the existence of language divisions in a multilingual society'. Besides, the fostering of the well-being of citizens and the provision of meaningful roles for them within the system can do much more to forge a sense of belonging and loyalty to the nation in spite of linguistic differences.[11]

The National Language Question

In the African context, national integration is often conceived in terms of facilitating communication links between diverse groups, mainly from different ethnic groups. Since, from the colonial period, education has played a major role in this effort, the European medium of education, which was also the official language, is considered the suitable instrument for integration. The point which is often missed in this approach is that the kind of integration made possible in this way is only horizontal integration which involves a combination of the segment of the educated elites from each of the different ethnic or linguistic groups in the country. This segment perhaps accounts for 10–15% of the total population. The question is whether national integration should be equated with integration of the elites. An alternative to this kind of integration is the one that links the elites with the masses. This is known as vertical integration. It is only through it that the vast majority of the people who have no access to the official language can ever hope to be involved in the system at some level or the other; and only an African language can make this sort of integration possible.

Commenting on the role of official languages, Thompson (1969: 361) says, 'It is doubtful . . . whether a European language is likely to become the most efficient nation-building instrument in many African states. European languages are still foreign to the African masses . . . To make one of them the sole official language in an African state is to prolong, perhaps to perpetuate, the horizontal cleavage which colonialism created in African societies, and thereby to impede rather than promote the growth of nationality.' The case can hardly be better put. But such is the preoccupation with foreign official languages that even when an African language is spoken by the majority of the population (e.g. Wolof in Senegal, Bambara in Mali, Hausa in Niger, Chichewa in Malawi), no one instinctively thinks of such African languages as the languages of national integration. Rather, the ready choice is the language of the former colonial power (in these cases, French or English). In effect, the interest of the educated elites who form a minority in each country is equated with the interest of the nation.

Closely bound up with the language of integration is the national language question.[12] Which specific language or languages should be adopted as a country's official language, its national language or both? The languages that are available to fill this role in Africa are:

1. A Language of Wider Communication (such as English, French, Spanish and Portuguese, which were the official European languages used in the colonial period).

2. Arabic, which is usually associated with Islam.

3. An indigenous African language, which can be a major language (such as Wolof in Senegal or Hausa in Niger), a minority language which has spread to a wider segment of the population (such as Krio in Sierra Leone),[13] an artificial language often conceived as uniting elements from different languages (such as the proposed Guosa in Nigeria).

4. An English-based Pidgin such as is found in Nigeria and Cameroon.

A number of factors have to be considered in deciding which language or languages should be adopted as a country's national or official language. The most important among these factors are: nationalism versus nationism, vertical integration, acceptability, population, language development status.[14]

Nationalism versus Nationism

According to Fishman (1968a), all nations have to apportion
attention and resources between 'the claims of authenticity' on
the one hand and the 'claims of efficiency' on the other. Claims
of authenticity correspond to the quest for nationalism, while
the claims of efficiency correspond to nationism. In terms of
language choice, nationalism, which involves sociocultural
integration and authenticity, calls for the adoption of an
indigenous language, while nationism, which is concerned with
political integration and efficiency, calls for any language that
can perform these functions. It would not matter at all if the
language is not indigenous. In fact, the chances are that it will
be a language already used in higher education and technology.
In balancing the conflicting claims of nationalism and
nationism, Fishman predicts that new nations are likely to
emphasize nationism rather than nationalism.

The language of nationism is one of the Languages of Wider
Communication (LWC's),[15] a term which presupposes the
existence of Languages of Narrower Communication (LNC's),
which is supposed to refer to such languages as Danish, Czech,
and Dutch which are not widely known among speakers of
other languages.[16] A Language of Wider Communication has
the advantage that, in most cases, it is already a *de facto*
language of government and higher education in which status it
is already deeply entrenched. This gives it the dominance that
is often justified by the international prestige of the language
as well as its association with technology.[17] Countries that are
interested in rapid development and modernization are believed
to gain a great deal by opting for a LWC, and individuals too
are supposed to realize that it confers advantages which a
sensible citizen can only ignore at his own peril. Williams (1986:
514) points out, in relation to the preference for English in
nineteenth-century Wales, that the slogan was, 'If you want to
get ahead, get an English head'.

In considering the prospects of language choice by developing
countries, Fishman (1971) divides the decisions by these
countries into three possible types:

1. *Type A decisions* are taken by countries that have no
   great tradition that the population can invoke to achieve
   integration. Such decisions are governed by a concern for
   nationism, and the choice is a LWC as a permanent national

symbol, for example Cameroon, Ghana, Gambia, Tanzania.

2. *Type B decisions* are taken by countries that have one great tradition, and hence language choice is governed by considerations of nationalism, leading to the choice of an indigenous language as a national language. However, since efficiency in the nation is also desirable, a LWC is often adopted as a transitional choice, as for instance in Ethiopia.

3. *Type C decisions* are taken by countries that have several great traditions. In view of the conflicting claims of these traditions, a compromise is required between national integration and ethnic identity. Such a compromise is best provided by a LWC which these countries are likely to opt for, for example India, Malaysia (no African example given).

In all the cases, and for the purposes of modernization, the nations are said to be likely to choose a LWC either as a permanent feature or as a transitional measure. By equating modernism with a LWC, Fishman clearly overplays the importance of such a language and ignores the strong nationalist claims for authenticity. If efficiency were all that mattered, there would be no persistent calls for the adoption of an African language as an official language. Tanzania had all the efficiency it needed in English; yet it chose Swahili as its national language, contrary to the prediction that it would choose a LWC in a Type A decision. The fact is that language is often seen as a vehicle for a people's culture, and a LWC, no matter how domesticated and Africanized, continues to be associated with a foreign culture.

Admittedly, reconciling the claims of nationalism and nationism will not be an easy matter. The choice of an indigenous language will involve language development and massive propagation, particularly among minority elements who may not readily accept the language chosen. On the other hand, retaining a LWC as the official language continues to favour only the educated elites and to lead to continued nationalist pressures for a language that can ensure mass participation in the national system. The likelihood seems to be that a LWC can only continue to be used for nationism as a transitional measure, while plans are pursued to achieve true national integration through an indigenous language or languages.

Vertical Integration

The point has been made earlier that the kind of integration made possible by a language policy which depends on a foreign official language is one between the elites of one ethnic group and the elites of other ethnic groups. While this facilitates communication and makes the business of governing possible, it limits participation to a fortunate few and excludes the masses who cannot participate because the language of government is not available to them. A national or official language must take seriously the need to bridge the gulf between the elites and the masses. There is a sharp contrast between those countries that have an indigenous national language and those that do not. The kind of grass-roots participation in political affairs which Swahili has made possible in Tanzania is in sharp contrast to the situation in Uganda, for example.

It appears that there are only two possible roads to vertical integration, and both are bound to involve massive investment in education. The first is to adopt the policy of spreading the language of the elites. This will mean trying both through the school system and mass literacy programmes to propagate a LWC. Considering the high figures of illiteracy in Africa, the fact that only a small proportion of children of school age actually succeed in going to school, and the resources required in terms of school expansion, teacher training and provision of materials, the task of spreading a LWC through the educational system appears to be an impossible one. The alternative is to build on a base of a language or languages already widely spoken. Although there are also costs involved, this task seems more feasible. The logic of vertical integration therefore points to the adoption of one or more indigenous languages.

Acceptability

In order to function as a truly national symbol, a language has to be acceptable to the different components of the country. In India, English was supposed to be replaced by Hindi fifteen years after independence. However, because of vehement opposition by non-Hindi-speaking groups, the requirement was suspended through the Language Legislation Act of 1967.[18] That is a pointer to what can happen when there is no acceptability.

The point is often made that those who are native speakers of the language selected to be a national language have an undue advantage and, to that extent, resentment may be felt by other groups and this could lead to a threat to national unity. This is the view represented by Nida and Wonderly (1971: 65) when they state the following in relation to pre-1963 Nigeria:

> In Nigeria, there is simply no politically neutral language. In fact, the division into three major regions reflects the three language poles: Hausa, Yoruba, Ibo. The political survival of Nigeria as a country would be even more seriously threatened than it is if any one of these three languages were promoted by the Government as being the one national language.[19]

In contrast to the alleged divisiveness of an indigenous language, a LWC is presented as a neutral language which could easily be adopted as a language of national unity or a compromise language. For example, Alexandre (1972: 87) claims that the colonial language is 'emotionally *neutral* since it belongs to no local tribe but rather can be common to peoples of different ethnic origins', and French educational policy-makers are reported to be of the view that 'French will serve the goals of African development because it will ensure unity as a *neutral* non-ethnic language and material development as a language of technology' (Weinstein 1980: 72). While it is true that a LWC does not belong to any ethnic group, it does not follow that it is therefore neutral and acceptable. All languages are culture-laden, and a LWC such as English or French carries with it the values of its native speakers which are shared in some ways by the elites in Africa. But it is also clear that the language does not 'unite' the elites, for, having used the language to unite to fight and win independence, they continue to use it for their ethnic and political rivalries and divisions.

It is because a LWC is not really neutral that demands continue to be made for an indigenous language of integration. Besides, acceptability is not an invariable factor. It can be engineered where the will to do so exists. Where a government is determined to carry out the necessary political and psychological campaign, language attitudes can be influenced. What is important is not to promote the language by itself as a symbol of unity, but to link it with other values and considerations. A case in point is the rapid spread of Hausa in Northern Nigeria between 1960 and 1967, which was linked to the 'northernization' policy of the then Northern Nigerian Government. In spite of political resistance by some of the non-Hausa/Fulani groups, the political integration of Northern Nigeria enhanced the speaking of the Hausa language as a lingua franca for the entire area. This was made possible by the linkage between the spread of the language and the political ideology of 'One North, One People' under which people of various ethnic and linguistic groups came to refer to themselves proudly as 'Northerners'.[20] The conclusion from this experience is that acceptability is also an 'ideologized' position which can be consciously promoted.

As a preliminary measure of likely acceptability, a survey of the indigenous languages in a country can be carried out to find out which languages are already being used as second languages by large segments of the population. The relative numbers involved as well as the geographical spread of such second language speakers could be a rough measure of acceptability.

Population

In determining the choice of a national language, population is usually an important factor. It is sometimes argued that there are two possible models: the majority model, by which the choice is based on the language of the majority of the population, and the minority model, by which the choice is based on the language of a minority of the population.

In debates on the national language question, it is sometimes suggested that the minority model is better because it puts most of the population at an equal disadvantage. The fear of domination will be allayed, as the minority speakers lack the superiority in numbers to lord it over the majority. Although this is a specious argument, the real problem concerns how a minority language is to be spread to the rest of the population, given that the pool of speakers from which to draw training expertise for teaching and language development activities is severely limited. The minority model, in so far as it may be said to exist, is no more than a historical fact arising from such factors as early written tradition and literary use of the minority language, strategic location and prestige of the speakers, and the use of the language as a trade language. Languages like Swahili in Tanzania or Krio in Sierra Leone were natively spoken by minorities. Today, Swahili has become a widespread lingua franca and national language, while Krio is rapidly spreading as a lingua franca and, in all probability, will emerge in the future as Sierra Leone's national language. For a minority language to become a national language, it must have acquired a majority of speakers, thereby ceasing, in effect, to be a minority language.

The majority model appears to be the only feasible model in contemporary policy formulation, unless a LWC is selected on the grounds that it already serves as an official language. Other things being equal, a language spoken by ten million people has a better chance of being adopted as a national language than one spoken by one million people.

The use of the population factor raises the entire question of how numbers of speakers are determined. The usual procedure is to make inferences from census figures which, in the African context, are based on ethnic affiliation and hardly ever include information on language. Thus, the 1963 census figures for Nigeria record 11.6 million Hausa and 4.7 million Fulani. However, it is well known that most of the Fulani speak Hausa as their only language and the rest are bilingual in Hausa and Fulfulde. A proper language census would have indicated this fact. This apart, language censuses in Africa are often politicized and geared narrowly to socio-economic questions (e.g. number of housing units, number of residents per unit, etc.). Quite often, the figures are unreliable because they have been grossly inflated in the expectation of the benefits that will accrue to each ethnic group in terms of resource allocation or political representation in various legislatures and councils.

Apart from the above problems, there are other general problems related to language questions in censuses. Questions such as 'What is your mother tongue?', 'What other language do you speak?', 'Which language do you know best?' are fraught with problems because of the vagueness in interpretation of 'mother tongue' (is it the first language or the home language?), 'speak' (to what degree and how often?) and 'know' (to what degree and how much use is made of it?). There is the notorious problem of the difficulty of making a clear-cut distinction between language and dialect, and the problem of respondents identifying with a larger ethnic group or putting emphasis on sub-ethnic differences. Finally, since most of the information from censuses involve self-reporting and assessment, the possibility of bias and unreliability of responses is always present.[21]

Language Development Status

It is a well-known fact that languages belong to different stages of development. While some have had a long literary tradition, others are just being reduced to writing. It is possible to estimate the stage of development in terms of such indices as use or non-use for normal written purposes (letters, newspapers, books), publication of original research in the sciences, translations of scientific work and level of standardization (Ferguson, 1962). Alternatively, the emphasis may be on national and international status, use as a school subject or medium, literary and religious uses (Stewart, 1968) or, more appropriately in the African context, the state of scientific study of the language (orthography, grammar and dictionary), publications (educational, literary and translations), use in mass media (including newspapers, magazines, radio and television) and use at different levels of education.[22] In an exercise based on these types of indices, Brann (1975) was able to quantify the language development status of 51 Nigerian languages, coming to the conclusion that Yoruba had the highest development index at 26, followed by Hausa at 25, Igbo at 23.5 and Efik at 20, a result which is hardly surprising since these are the languages taught as subjects in secondary schools and offered in the secondary school certificate examination. This kind of rough test can be used to determine the language development status of other African languages.

Employing the six criteria of nationism, nationalism, vertical integration, acceptability, population and language development status, it is now possible to consider the prospects of the five types of languages that are possible candidates for a national language. As a starting-point the presence or absence of each of these features may be indicated as in Table 1.1.

A Language of Wider Communication has the positive advantage that it is already being used internationally, particularly for higher education and technology. To that extent, it has an advantage over the other types. In terms of development, it also ranks highest by virtue of its use in a greater range of domains and the enormous technical and literary texts available in it. On the other hand, it does not fulfil the requirements of authenticity, nor can it help in achieving integration between the elites and the masses. Its acceptability depends on the particular situation of the country concerned.

Table 1.1. Rating of language types

	Nationism	Nationalism	Vertical Integration	Acceptability	Population	Lang. dev status
1 LWC	+	–	–	±	–	+
2 Arabic	–	+	+	±	+	+
3 Indigenous language						
a) Major	–	+	+	±	+	+
b) Minority	–	+	–	–	–	–
c) Artificial	–	–	–	–	–	–
4 Pidgin	–	+	+	–	–	–

While there are elements that will welcome its continued dominance on grounds either of entrenched privileges or fear of another language being selected, there are others that continue to find it unacceptable on nationalist grounds.

Arabic is already being widely used in several domains, but to the extent that, even in the more advanced Arab countries, recourse is still had to a LWC for technological and industrial development, it must be marked as 'minus' under nationism. It is already well developed, ranking, however, lower than a LWC in this regard. Its acceptability, of course, depends on the situation of each country. Where the country is an Islamic one, there is usually no problem about the adoption of Arabic, provided it is widely spoken in the country. For example, Arabic is the national and official language of Mauritania; but in Sudan, where it also has the same status, there are problems because of religious and ethnic differences between the North and South. In effect, Arabic functions truly as a national and official language only for Northern Sudan. Given population, therefore, and Islamic culture, Arabic fulfils the requirements of both nationalism and vertical integration.

A major indigenous African language cannot compete with a LWC in terms of its use for modernization and, with perhaps the exception of Somali, ranks even below Arabic in terms of language development. Its acceptability will also depend on the situation in the country concerned; but being a major language, it has population in its favour and its most important attributes are that it satisfies the requirement of both authenticity and vertical integration.

A minority language, being indigenous, conforms to the demand for authenticity. However, lacking the population to back it, it cannot fulfil the requirements of vertical integration and acceptability. Needless to say, it is likely to have low language development status; hence its use for modernization does not even arise.

The notion that an artificial language can be created from a composite of several languages is one which sounds attractive to those who are genuinely worried about the so-called disadvantages of multilingualism, but are completely naive about language structure and language as a system. In this respect, there is perhaps some confusion between standardization of *dialects* of the same language, in the carrying out of which it is possible to evolve a standard from several dialects, and inventing an artificial language from a composite of different *languages*. For example, standard Shona in Zimbabwe was evolved from the Zezuru, Karanga, Korekore, Manyika and Ndau dialects.[23] Similarly, the so-called Union Igbo in Nigeria was formed from the Onitsha, Owerri, Bonny and Arochukwu dialects, an enterprise that resulted in failure because speakers of Igbo rejected it. An artificial language fails on each of the criteria for the selection of a national language. Its chances of being adopted are, therefore, nil.

Pidgin is an attractive candidate for national language status. It does not suffer from the elitism associated with English; hence, it satisfies both the requirement of authenticity and vertical integration. It has major drawbacks, however. First, its language development status is almost non-existent (there are no serious books, for instance, written in pidgin and even the writing of the language is still subject to a great deal of inconsistency as well as confusion with English orthography). Second, there is no large population to back it. (In Nigeria, for example, pidgin is the unofficial language of the armed forces and the police; it is also spoken in the coastal areas as well as in some urban centres, but it is virtually unknown in large areas of the country.) Third, due to its restricted use it is likely to be unacceptable. Fourth, since English is still required for nationism, and pidgin cannot function in that role, it is often argued that English might as well be retained rather than exchanged for an English-based pidgin.

It should be clear from the above that the three serious candidates for national language status in the African context are a LWC, Arabic (in an Islamic country) and a major indigenous African language. Ranking of the three will depend on the weighting given to each of the criteria, and, as has been pointed out earlier, it may well be that a combination of a major African language or Arabic and a LWC in complementary roles is inevitable as a transitional arrangement.

Official Languages

In looking at the actual situation of national and official languages in Africa, it is perhaps more useful, and certainly more revealing, to concentrate on *official languages*. This is because a country may declare a language as its national language and not use it at all in any serious official capacity. For example, although Kenya's national language is Swahili,

its official language, which is used for administration and
education, is English. Besides, a Language of Wider Communication is never called a national language; therefore, the
only basis for comparing it with other languages is to look at
the situation of official languages.

Broadly speaking, there are two major types of situation:
sole official languages and joint official languages, with further
differentiation according to the types of languages involved:

    1. *Sole official languages.*
       (a) Language of Wider Communication:
          (i) *English.* (Gambia, Sierra Leone, Liberia, Ghana,
               Nigeria, Uganda, Kenya, Malawi, Zambia,
               Zimbabwe, Swaziland, Mauritius, Seychelles);
          (ii) *French.* (Guinea Republic, Senegal, Mali, Niger,
               Chad, Burkina Faso, Côte d'Ivoire, Togo,
               Benin, Central African Republic, Congo, Gabon,
               Zaire);
          (iii) *Portuguese.* (Guinea Bissau, Sao Tome and
               Principe, Cape Verde, Angola, Mozambique);
          (iv) *Spanish.* (Equatorial Guinea).
       (b) Arabic: (Mauritania, Sudan).
       (c) Major African Language:
          (i) Somali (Somalia);
          (ii) Amharic (Ethiopia).
    2. *Joint official languages.*
       (a) LWC and Another Language:
          (i) French and Arabic (Djibouti, Comoros);
          (ii) English and Major African Language:
               Swahili (Tanzania)
               Sotho (Lesotho)
               Tswana (Botswana)
          (iii) French and Major African Language:
               Kirundi (Burundi)
               Kinyarwanda (Rwanda)
               Malagasy (Madagascar)
       (b) LWC and LNC:
          French and English (Cameroon).

The distribution of the official languages either as sole or
joint official languages is indicated in Table 1.2.

Table 1.2. Distribution of official languages

French —	19
English —	17
Major African language	8
Portuguese —	5
Arabic —	4
Spanish —	1
Total No. of Countries =	45
Total No. of Countries × No. of Official languages =	54

The picture that emerges from the above profile is that the situation reflects largely the colonial history of each country. With minor exceptions, the language of the colonial powers continues to be either a sole or joint official language. The case of Cameroon, which was formerly administered by the French (East Cameroon) and the English (West Cameroon), demonstrates clearly this pattern, as the two colonial languages have survived as official languages. This reality is a measure of the magnitude of the problem of breaking with the past and making a new policy decision on language choice.

Notwithstanding the existing patterns of official languages, there are nationalist attitudes expressed in demands for change in the direction of a definite policy of encouraging the evolution of an indigenous national and official language. Such attitudes, in turn, invite a reaction ranging from indifference to outright hostility. In debates on the national language question, three approaches are discernible: status quo, radical and gradualist.

The status quo approach is that which tends in the direction of nationism. The typical arguments for this approach go as follows: Our country is a young one faced with many problems, particularly those of rapid economic development, better education, and technological advance. Any language that can make it possible for us to attain these goals in the shortest possible time is welcome. In any case, we already have an official language which has been serving us well. Some say it is a foreign language, but a language that we have been using for so long and in which we have produced creative writing should cease to be seen as a foreign language. It has made inter-ethnic co-operation possible and it has also facilitated our access to the international world of science and technology. We should continue to use it, rather than bring problems on our heads by trying to make a difficult, if not impossible, decision as to which of our many languages is to be our national language.

The arguments advanced in support of the status quo approach are superficial because they ignore the claims of sentimental attachment and authenticity. The continued use of a foreign official language will leave the gap between the elites and the masses as wide as ever. Even where governments have been inclined to this approach, they have found it politically inexpedient to come out openly and say so. This is why no African country has proclaimed a LWC as its national language; rather, the formula has been to say that English or French is only an official language, and that the search for a national language still continues.

The radical approach tends in the direction of nationalism. The arguments for it go as follows: For a long time, we have talked about having a national language without doing anything about it. The more we delay, the greater is the danger that we will lose the will to change. Thus, we will have a foreign national language as the symbol of our nationality, and this language with its associations with a foreign culture will cut the majority of our people off from participation in the national system. It is true that our languages may not be well developed yet for higher education and technology, but they will never be, unless we decide to use them. A decision should therefore be made in favour of a national language and immediate steps taken to develop and spread its use in a wide range of domains.

Again, the arguments advanced in favour of the radical approach oversimplify the problems involved in having a viable national language. A radical decision taken without adequate consideration of implementation procedures will remain merely a decision on paper. Besides, the situation of the country has to be such as to make a radical decision feasible. The only country in Africa south of the Sahara that has been able to make such a radical decision and get away with it is Somalia, which decided in favour of Somali in 1972 with a revolutionary proclamation stating that '[t]he Somali language will be adopted, starting from today, as the only official language of the country'.[24] The case of Tanzania, which decided in favour of Swahili as its national language in 1961, can also be cited, but this was definitely not as revolutionary as the Somali decision, since

English was retained in a transitional role as a complementary official language.[25]

The radical approach is not feasible in most African countries. For it to succeed, the language chosen must be one that is already widely spoken either as a first or second language; there must be the political will and mobilization of the people to support the policy; and there must be a strong or revolutionary government to give the necessary impetus and backing to the formulation and implementation of the policy. It is only in this type of context that the enormous language planning activities needed to make the policy a reality can be effectively embarked upon and achieved. Even so, the implications of a radical approach for higher education in particular are perhaps treated lightly or totally ignored.

The gradualist approach tries to achieve a compromise between the nationalist consideration of having an indigenous language for authenticity and the nationist requirement for a language for running the country in an efficient manner. The arguments for it go as follows: The adoption of a foreign language as our national language is not justified. On the other hand, an immediate decision on an indigenous language is not a feasible proposition, partly because there may not be an obvious choice, and, even if there is, considerable work needs to be done to develop the language and take necessary steps to spread it. In view of this, a long-term view has to be taken of the matter. While steps are going on to evolve an indigenous national language or languages, the foreign language currently serving as an official language should continue to serve in that role.

The logic of the situation in most African countries leaves one with no other choice but the gradualist approach. If properly implemented, it will avoid unnecessary disruption and upheaval, while ultimately ensuring that the desired nationalist goal is attained. The danger with the approach is that it may become a cover for the status quo approach. Without adequate steps being taken, the transitional arrangement for a foreign official language may become a permanent situation, with any prospect of change being seen as difficult, unnecessary, and perhaps even impossible.

Notes to Chapter 1

1. The conflict theory of integration of plural societies is favoured by most social scientists. See in particular Mazrui (1969), Van den Berge (1969) and Freeman (1974).
2. Many of these measures are discussed in Smock and Bentsi-Enchill (1975: 3–17).
3. For a discussion of the problems of associating language with 'tribe', see Hymes (1968).
4. Haarman (1986) makes this point very strongly in referring to factors such as cultural heritage, ancestry, language and self-identification.
5. For comments on this, see Deutsch (1963) and Gellar (1973). The title of one of the chapters in Alexandre (1972) is 'From Tribes to Nations: Problems of Communication'.
6. This point is made by Colson (1968: 201–2) and Gellar (1973: 388–9).
7. Note that these two were listed as separate languages in the list of nine languages approved for education in post-independence Ghana. See Agyei (n.d.).
8. See Kelman (1971).
9. Information on languages and percentages of speakers is drawn mainly from International African Institute (1981), Okonkwo (1975) and Mann and Dalby (1987).
10. For example, following a proposal by Capo, the cluster Fon, Gun, Adja, Watchi, Aizo, Mina are now accepted as one language, Gbe. See Capo (1988).
11. For an elaboration of this point, see Kelman (1971: 27).
12. The term 'national language' is often used in different senses. It could refer to any language native to a country, any language native to a country and given some measure of recognition by the government, or any language native to a country and recognized by the government as an instrument for achieving sociocultural integration, particularly at the national level. It is in this last sense (see Fishman 1971: 32) that the term is used in this study. An official language is, of course, the language of administration and of education at some levels. A national language only assumes an important role when it is also being used as an official language.
13. Note that a creole is considered here to be an indigenous language because of its origin, and also because it is spoken as a mother tongue.
14. For earlier discussions of some of the factors see Spencer (1963), Banjọ (1975) and Bamgboṣe (1977).
15. The term Languages of Wider Communication (LWC) was introduced by Fishman (1968a) and has now gained wide currency in sociolinguistics.
16. See Kloss (1969).
17. Some rationalizations for the dominance of LWCs are discussed in Kotey (1975).
18. A detailed discussion of the Indian case is presented in Dua (1985).

19. The Nigerian situation has, of course, changed a great deal since 1963. In addition to the original three regions, one more was created in August 1963; the four regions were split into twelve states in 1967; seven more states were created in 1975, and two more in 1987, making a total of twenty-one states.
20. For a discussion of the role of Hausa in the political integration of Northern Nigeria, see Paden (1968).
21. Some of the general problems of language questions in censuses are discussed in Lieberson (1966) and McConnell (1979), and the notorious vagueness of 'mother tongue' is extensively reviewed in Pattanayak (1981: 47–65).
22. Some information along these lines is provided for major African languages and official languages in International African Institute (1981).
23. Information given by Ansre (1971: 681).
24. The information on this declaration is attributed to the Somali National Language Commission and quoted in Kashoki (1982: 19).
25. Further information on the declaration of Swahili as Tanzania's national language and some of the steps taken to implement the policy can be found in Abdulaziz (1971) and Whiteley (1968).

2

Language, Communication and National Development

Multilingualism and National Development

National development is usually described in terms of economic growth, attainment of economic targets, growth rate, increase in Gross National Product (GNP) or Gross Domestic Product (GDP), rise in *per capita* income, etc. It is, of course, possible to make a detailed breakdown of such indicators of national development, as Allardt (1973: 268–71) has done in terms of: societal allocations, embracing allocations to different sectors of the economy (industry, defence, education, technology, administration, communication, etc.); societal goals, embracing economic prosperity and growth as expressed in *per capita* and employment rates, political efficiency, political participation and modernization efforts; and individual goals, embracing level of welfare as expressed in private consumption and housing, life expectancy, freedom to choose jobs or belong to organizations. Whichever way this concept of national development is amplified, it is to be considered a narrow one in the sense that it equates national development with socio-economic development.

Even assuming the narrow conception of national development, a question arises about the role of language in socio-economic development. The assumption is that language does have a role to play, but the nature of that role is hardly spelt out. One major problem, however, to which attention has been drawn, is the relationship between linguistic heterogeneity and development. Linguistically heterogeneous states are said to be characterized by low or very low *per capita* GNP and are usually economically underdeveloped, while linguistically homogeneous states have a high or medium *per capita* GNP and are relatively economically well-developed (Banks and Textor 1965). Fishman (1968b), making use of the Banks and Textor cross-polity files, has shown that there is no necessary correlation between linguistic heterogeneity and low economic status or vice versa. Of the 114 countries examined, 52 are linguistically homogeneous, while 62 are heterogeneous. Of the 52 homogeneous countries, 25 (or about 50%) have low or very low *per capita* GNP, while 47 of the 62 heterogeneous countries (about 75%) have low or very low *per capita* GNP. All the countries in Africa, with the exception of South Africa, belong to the category of low or very low *per capita* GNP; and these include not only the lingusitically homogeneous Arab countries of North Africa, but also homogeneous black countries such as Burundi, Rwanda, Somalia and Madagascar. Clearly, this evidence suggests that there must be other variables at work. Whatever may be responsible for the economic plight of the poorer countries, the crucial variable certainly cannot possibly be language.

In spite of the above, heterogeneity continues to be viewed as a deficiency or disadvantage. As Pool (1972: 214) has put it, 'it is said that language diversity slows down economic development, by, for example, breaking occupational mobility, reducing the number of people available for mobilization into the modern sector of the economy, decreasing efficiency and preventing the diffusion of innovative techniques'. Even Fishman, while rejecting a correlation between linguistic heterogeneity and underdevelopment, concluded that sectionalism and the presence of politically unassimilated minorities are two distinguishing characteristics of linguistic heterogeneity, and obviously, these would be seen as impediments to national integration and national development.[1]

Homogeneity of modern states, whether linguistic or ethnic, is a myth. In a survey of 132 states, Connor (1972: 320) found only 12 (9.1%) that could be described as ethnically homogeneous. An additional 25 states (18.9%) contain an ethnic group which accounts for 90% of the state's population, and in a further 25 states, the largest element constitutes between 75% and 89% of the total population. In 31 states (23.5%), the largest ethnic group does not account for more than 50% to 74% of the population, and in 39 states (29.5%) the largest group does not even account for half of the population of the state. Taking a cut-off point of 90% to determine homogeneity, the situation is that even if one stretches the meaning of homogeneity, not more than 28% of all the states can be said to be homogeneous. The norm, therefore, for contemporary states is heterogeneity, which becomes more striking still when ethnic diversity within states is taken into consideration. For instance, Connor found that the number of distinct ethnic groups in some states runs into hundreds and that in as many as 53 states (40.2% of the total number of states) there are at least five different units into which the population can be divided. National development, even when narrowly defined as socio-economic development, therefore has to take place largely in the context of linguistic and ethnic heterogeneity.

Literacy, Mass Communication and National Development

There are at least two areas in which language is crucial to national development, even in its restricted definition as socio-economic development: literacy and communication.

Three aspects of literacy inevitably link it directly with socio-economic development: correlation between illiteracy and poverty, literacy and socio-economic transformation (including development of new skills and change in attitudes and life-style), and literacy and economic growth.

The UNESCO review of literacy in the world since the 1965 Teheran Conference draws the firm conclusion: 'Illiteracy has a close correlation with poverty. In the twenty-five least developed countries, where the *per capita* product is less than \$100 a year, illiteracy rates are over 80%.'[2] Besides, countries with the highest illiteracy rates are also shown to have higher population growth rates.

The adult illiteracy situation in the world around 1970 corresponds largely to the cleavage between the developed and developing countries.

As Table 2.1 shows, the highly industrialized and economically advanced countries of Europe and North America have the lowest illiteracy rates, while Africa tops the illiteracy rate at 73.7%, which is about 211% of the world average. Projections into the 1980s reveal virtually the same position, with the world at 28.9% and Africa at 60.6%.[3]

A similar picture emerges when the reverse situation of literacy rates is examined across countries in the five regions of the world: Africa, America, Asia, Europe and Oceania (see Table 2.2).[4]

The top bracket of literacy rates at 81–100% shows clearly the relative position of the regions: the number of countries in Europe in this bracket is 90%, and the corresponding figures for the other regions are America 81%, Oceania 77%, Asia 30% and

Table 2.1. Adult illiteracy percentage around 1970

World	34.2
Developing countries	
Africa	73.7
Latin America	23.6
Asia	46.8
Developed countries	
North America	1.5
Europe	3.6
Oceania	10.3

Source: Unesco (1972: 22)

Africa 4%. Although these figures are obscured by the dilution of developing and developed countries, particularly in America and Oceania, the obvious conclusion from the Table is still that the more literate the population of a country is, the more developed it is likely to be. The regions with the best developed countries, for example Europe, America (with the major position of the United States and Canada), Oceania (with the position of Australia and New Zealand), have the highest literacy rates in the top bracket, while Asia and Africa, with the largest number of developing countries, lag very much behind. As usual, Africa is in the least favourable position. It seems clear, then, that Africa's socio-economic underdevelopment problem cannot be solved without improved literacy. The observation that 'illiteracy cannot be dissociated from its development context any more than it can be from its demographic context'[5] is therefore very apt. As we shall see, literacy in the African context must mean paying more attention to indigenous languages as an effective means of eradicating illiteracy.

Experience with literacy work, particularly functional literacy, has shown that it is a powerful means of developing new skills. For example, it enables the peasant farmer to gain knowledge of the use of fertilizers, use of credit, marketing and price trends and other techniques; it helps the industrial worker to convert from old to new plants, and from being unskilled to skilled, and thus to improve production; it makes possible the training of women for employment not only in small-scale and cottage industries but also in matters pertaining to health, family

Table 2.2 Adult literacy rates: distribution according to countries and regions

Regions	Number of countries	Literacy rates				
		0-20%	21-40%	41-60%	61-80%	81-100%
Africa	54	14	19	14	5	2
America	47	0	1	3	5	38
Asia	40	3	8	6	11	12
Europe	40	0	0	0	4	36
Oceania	17	0	1	2	1	13

Source: Calculated from The Economist (1987: 18)

planning, etc., thus leading to an improvement in maternal and child health and combating population explosion.[6]

An assessment of the Experimental World Literacy Programme (Unesco 1976b) has also shown that attitudes can be radically transformed as a result of literacy training. Launched in 1966, the programme became operational in 1969 and was completed in 1973. It covered eleven countries: Algeria, Ecuador, Ethiopia, Guinea, India, Iran, Madagascar, Mali, Sudan, Syria, and Tanzania. Part of the assessment was designed to test how well integrated participants had become in terms of ability to plan, communicate and obtain information, and participate in societal activities; how much better they were in terms of skills and working habits as well as ability to adopt new practices; how their socio-economic life had been transformed, leading to improved standards of living and attitudes conducive to development. The results of the assessment were as indicated in Table 2.3.

These figures show clearly that the influence of literacy on socio-economic development is overwhelmingly positive. Hence, a further case is made for the eradication of illiteracy in order to achieve national development in its narrow sense. It is not surprising, therefore, to see a conscious linking of literacy to rural development projects as well as agricultural and industrial development. Countries in Africa which are reported to have combined their literacy campaigns with development projects include Gabon, Niger, Burkina Faso, Ghana, Mali, Nigeria, Kenya and Zambia.[7]

Although there is a paucity of data linking literacy to economic growth, we have the example of MOBRAL (The Brazilian Adult Literacy Experiment), which was created in 1967 and began operation in 1970. In Brazil, yearly growth rates in GDP in the years 1962–7 were reported to be 3.7%. These rates soared to an average of 10.1% in 1968–74. The

Table 2.3. Literacy and socio-economic impact

Influence	Integration	Know-how	Transformation
Positive	72	88	86
None	9	3	3
Negative	19	9	11

Source: Adapted from Unesco (1976b: 56)

period that saw a phenomenal rise in growth rates coincided with expansion in education, including adult literacy.[8] The adult illiteracy rate in Brazil in 1970 was 33.8%, with a total illiterate population of 18.1 million aged 15 and above. By 1976, the rate had dropped to 24.3% with a total illiterate population of 15.6 million aged 15 and above. It is obvious, however, that the improvement in economic growth rates cannot be attributed solely to literacy; for current figures for Brazil show that the adult illiteracy rate as of 1980 is 25.5% (that is, higher than in 1976), and the total adult illiterate population aged 15 and above is 18.7 million (higher than in 1970).[9] The reason for this situation, which is typical of that in most developing countries, is that the population is increasing at a much faster rate than the literacy programmes can cope with.

Attention has been drawn to the fallacy of assuming a facile and direct correlation between more education and greater economic development (Dore, 1976; Adams, 1977). However, it is not denied, even by those critical of this position, that there are aspects of education that do indeed support economic growth. For example, literacy appears to be one aspect of education that has consistently been accepted as being relevant to improved economic performance.

Communication in the sense of the mass media is also directly relevant to national development. At its most elementary level, communication can ensure a flow of information on various aspects of a country's socio-economic life. For example, in agriculture, it could disseminate information on fertilizers, pesticides, high-yield varieties of crops, appropriate planting seasons, irrigation and preservation as well as marketing outlets. In health programmes, it could provide information on environmental sanitation, nutrition, preventive measures, first aid, immunization, family planning, ante-natal and child care, etc. In rural and community development, it could give appropriate guidance on how to set up and run local projects, where to seek assistance and necessary inputs, how to organize co-operatives and similar associations. The media also represent a powerful instrument in ensuring political mobilization in order to ensure full participation by the populace in political and development programmes, particularly through a sustained programme of civic education. In short, as Schramm (1964: 43–4) puts it, an increased flow of information in a developing nation provides a *climate* for national development. 'It makes expert knowledge available where it is needed, and provides a forum for discussion, leadership, and decision making. It helps to raise the general level of aspiration.' Although the media are also open to manipulation under dictatorial and tyrannical governments, this is a risk worth taking in view of the beneficial uses of the media under benevolent governments whose major concern is the welfare of their citizens.

In a study of two Indian villages, Kothuru and Pathuru, Rao (1966) found a reciprocal relationship between communication and economic development. The more modern village, Kothuru, was better developed than the traditional village of Pathuru, and hence attracted a greater flow of information. For example, it had 28 copies of newspapers circulating in the village as opposed to five in the other village, 10 radio sets as compared to four in the traditional village, 30 listeners to the community radio set as opposed to six in the other village. The net result of all this was that the greater flow of information in the modern village opened it to greater outside influences, increased knowledge and greater economic activity, with the resultant increase in economic development. From this study, Rao concludes that the role of communication in a developing community is very wide. In the economic sphere, it helps citizens to find alternative ways of making a living, raises the family's economic status, creates demand for goods and thus stimulates production, and widens the base of those engaged in sponsoring enterprises. In the social sphere, it aids the attainment of status based on merit rather than birth or traditional position, motivates the illiterate to become literate, helps to induce parents to see the value of educating their children, and fosters a respect for human dignity. In the political sphere, it widens the scope of mass participation, disseminates information about government programmes, enables the government to get feedback on such programmes, and generally strengthens the forces of unity and integration.[10] Given the high rates of illiteracy in most of the developing countries, it is obvious that the mass media can only effectively reach the masses through the local languages. In fact, in the Indian case, the villagers listened to radio programmes and read newspapers in Urdu and Telugu.

In the foregoing sections, it is argued that national development, even if narrowly conceived in terms of socio-economic goals, has relevance for language, particularly in terms of such agents of development as literacy and communication. This argument may be taken further by insisting that national development cannot be limited in scope to socioeconomic development. A wider and more satisfactory conception of national development is that which sees it as total human development. In this model of development, the emphasis is on a full realization of the human potential and a maximum utilization of the nation's resources for the benefit of all.

The primacy of man as the source of all economic development is a point which Schumacher (1973) has effectively made. It is man, he says, who provides the primary resource and 'the key factor of all economic development comes out of the mind of man'. However, a crucial factor in this creativity is education, the essence of which is the transmission of values. Although poverty may be traced to material factors such as lack of natural wealth, capital or infrastructure, those factors are entirely secondary. The primary causes of poverty are really deficiencies in education, organization and discipline. It is these, rather than material goods, that can stimulate development, as can be shown by economic miracles achieved by countries without material resources but with the crucial factors of education, organization and discipline intact. Hence, development cannot be created, bought, ordered or transferred. The crucial factors have to become a property of not just a few but of the whole society.

The conclusion by Schumacher which is most relevant for our purpose is that looking at development in quantitative terms such as GNP, investment and savings is not really useful for developing countries:

> Economic development is something much wider and
> deeper than economics, let alone econometrics. Its roots
> lie outside the economic sphere, in education,
> organization, discipline, and, beyond that, in political
> independence and a national consciousness of self-reliance
> . . . It can succeed only if it is carried forward as a broad,
> popular 'movement of reconstruction' with primary
> emphasis on the full utilization of the drive, enthusiasm,
> intelligence, and labour power of everyone.[11]

To do otherwise is to follow a course that must lead to failure.

The man-centredness and human face of development are now increasingly accepted as the correct path to development.

In the words of former President Julius Nyerere of Tanzania:
> In the Third World we talk a great deal about economic
> development -- about expanding the number of goods and
> services, and the capacity to produce them. But the goods
> are needed to serve men; services are required to make the
> lives of men more easeful as well as more fruitful.
> Political, social, and economic organization is needed to
> enlarge the freedom and dignity of men. Always we come
> back to Man -- to Liberated Man -- as the purpose of
> activity, the purpose of development. So development is
> for man, by Man and of Man.[12]

The Declaration of Persepolis which emerged from the International Symposium for Literacy held at Persepolis, Iran, 3–8 September 1975, also came out strongly in favour of man-based development in declaring that literacy is not merely acquiring the skills of reading, writing and arithmetic, but 'a contribution to the liberation of man and his full development'. It should stimulate initiative, and encourage participation with a view to achieving 'authentic human development'.[13]

Aid donors are often accused of being insensitive to local requirements and transmitting technology as though it could be transplanted unmodified from one environment to another in a binary relationship in which the West is the generator of technology and aid-giver, and the Third World the consumer and aid-getter.[14] The picture now is changing fast to the extent that aid-givers are now in the forefront of stressing the need to adapt and transform foreign technology in consonance with the social and cultural situation of each country. For example, Article 10 of the 3rd African-Caribbean-Pacific Countries (ACP)/ European Economic Commission (EEC) Convention states specifically:
> Cooperation shall be aimed at supporting development in
> the ACP states, a process centred on man himself and
> rooted in each people's culture. It shall back up the
> policies and measures adopted by those States to enhance
> their human resources, increase their own creative
> capacities and promote their cultural identities.
> Cooperation shall also encourage participation by the
> population in the design and execution of development
> operations.[15]

Inspired by Schumacher, Ansre (1976) has proposed four elements relevant to an overall national development: economic development, politico-judicial development, sociocultural development and intellectual and educational development. In all this, he claims that the role of language is crucial since in wealth-getting and wealth-sharing, a minority official language cannot produce the best results. At best, it will only produce a wealthy few. On the other hand, a language shared by many should ensure greater productivity and fairer distribution. Similarly, law is only just and meaningful if the language in which it is couched is accessible to all. Sociocultural development obviously points to indigenous languages, while even intellectual and educational development needs to have its roots in the language of the community.

A summary of the elements that should go into national development as defined in a broader sense include the following:

1. Integrated development in which economic development is linked to social and cultural development, and the combination of all three is designed to improve the condition of man in society.

2. Self-reliance as the basis of all development instead of mass importation of expertise.

3. Intellectual aid as a surer basis of development in preference to material aid.[16]

4. Technology whenever transferred to be domesticated and indigenized to conform with the sociocultural norms and conditions of the country.

5. Mass participation and grass-roots involvement in order to ensure widespread and genuine development.

In the light of an examination of national development in its narrow and broad senses, we are now in a position to consider the role of language. As usual, two models present themselves: the model of use of official languages, usually LWCs, and the model of use of indigenous languages.

Given that the development effort aims to reach the masses, it is obvious that the language to be used in literacy and communication, for example, must be one that is capable of reaching the vast proportion of the population. In literacy education, pride of place has usually belonged to indigenous languages. Earlier attempts to use foreign official languages, such as French in Mali[17] or English for tobacco growers in Western Nigeria, ended in dismal failure. Among the African countries that have a vigorous programme of literacy in African languages are Mali, Togo, Somalia, Tanzania, Nigeria, Guinea,

Niger, Burundi and Zambia. The advantages of such media are that forms and knowledge of values of the culture are better learnt and transmitted, the positive attitude to language encourages greater motivation to learn, the course of instruction is psychologically more adequate as the concepts are already familiar, and the choice of language is in consonance with cultural and political attitudes.[18]

Similarly, in the area of mass communication, the undoubted advantages that can be achieved through a greater flow of information necessarily call for an intensification of the use of African languages in the media. Unfortunately, communication specialists tend to play down the role of such languages. For example, Schramm (1964: 101–2) sees Africa as 'a veritable crazy quilt of languages', the use of which inevitably makes for small audiences. By contrast, he suggests that the use of Spanish in Latin America and Portuguese in Brazil may have facilitated the growth of the press, while in India the use of regional and tribal languages increases the problems of national broadcasting and exchange of information. Similarly, Weiner (1967: 192) sees multiplicity of languages as a barrier to communication, and particularly the development of Indian tribal languages as divisive, since literacy leads to a deepening of divisions in terms of reading materials. The familiar bogy of linguistic heterogeneity and its alleged disadvantages are seen at work here again. The point which is often ignored is that the logic of mass participation points to not less, but increased use of the many languages available in a country in order to reach the widest possible segment of the community.

A similar indifference to the importance of indigenous languages is shown in the compilation of the statistics of books published in African countries. The Unesco Statistical Yearbook 1987 puts together under 'National Language' publications in foreign official languages and African languages. It is only by studying the footnotes that the following picture (Table 2.4) emerges for the few African countries (south of the Sahara) represented in the survey.

By separating titles which have been lumped together under the heading 'National Language', we can now see that, in almost all cases, publication in the foreign official language far outstrips that in the indigenous languages. Rwanda is the only country in which publication in Kinyarwanda is greater than in French. In Angola, Senegal, Mauritius and Mozambique,

Table 2.4. Book production by language[19]

Country	Year	Indigenous language	Foreign official language	
Angola	1985	—	47	Portuguese
Ethiopia	1985	24	131	English
Ghana	1983	38	312	English
Madagascar	1984	114	199	French
Malawi	1984	53	55	English
Mali	1983	28	63	French
Mauritius	1985	1	48/29	English/French
Mozambique	1984	1	42	Portuguese
Reunion	1985	3	64	French
Rwanda	1985	12	2	French
Senegal	1983	—	42	French
Zimbabwe	1985	98	444	English
	Total	282	1,478	

Source: Unesco (1987)

publication in indigenous languages is practically non-existent. Production in African languages represents only 16% of total book production.

In the area of communication, we are confronted with a similar problem. Opubor (1973) draws attention to the fact that media content in Nigeria is oriented towards the elite, that on radio and television news bulletins in English are three times as long as the equivalent in any other language, and that media coverage in minority languages is virtually non-existent. Of course, the situation may have changed somewhat with the creation of more states and the growing importance of hitherto non-major languages. But even so, the dominance of English is still to be seen in news broadcasts, special features and documentaries, talks, and political and public service broadcasts on government activities.

A look at the content of radio broadcasts in some selected African countries will show how crucial the matter of the language of news dissemination and other programmes is (Table 2.5).

All the radio stations in the five countries are government-owned, but the ideological complexion of the government manifests itself in the choice of content. For example, religious programmes do not exist in the socialist republics of Benin, Congo and Ethiopia; and the combined information and education programmes feature highly in Benin (60.2%), Congo (43.2%), Ethiopia (64.3%) and Ghana (61.6%). Along with that of entertainment and cultural programmes, the content of radio programmes in these countries points to an enhanced use of indigenous languages. For how can government information and rural development training be disseminated in the rural areas other than through the local language? The Unesco compilation of 1975 on world communications is remarkable in this respect in showing an awareness of the importance of the use of African languages in newspapers, radio and television. Not only does it list African languages in which newspapers and journals are published, it gives, where possible, circulation figures. It also lists languages used in broadcasting, sometimes giving information about the number of hours of transmission and the percentage of the target population reached. To give a few examples, the publication says that by broadcasting in English and Tswana, Radio Botswana is able to reach 90% of the population. In Burundi, three bi-weekly journals are

Table 2.5. Radio broadcasts: programmes by function

	Benin (1981)	Botswana (1985)	Congo (1983)	Ethiopia (1985)	Ghana (1985)
Total annual broadcast hours:	5,331	6,205	5,757	6,180	11,597
Types of broadcast by percentage:					
Informative programmes (including news)	47.0	16.2	23.9	30.6	43.4
Educational programmes (including rural development)	13.2	15.6	19.3	33.7	18.2
Cultural programmes	6.8	2.9	13.3	7.3	0.8
Religious programmes	—	3.1	—	—	2.8
Advertisements	9.3	—	0.2	0.3	1.6
Entertainment	22.6	42.9	30.7	28.1	29.4
Other	1.1	19.3	12.5	—	3.8

Source: Unesco (1987)

published -- two in Kirundi with a circulation of 45,000 and one in French with a circulation of 1,500. In Ghana, the Ghana Broadcasting Corporation Network I (GBC I) broadcasts for thirteen hours daily carrying general programmes, news, and all important ministerial announcements in Ghanaian languages, and in Kenya, there is a local language network broadcasting in eighteen languages, including Kikuyu, Masai, Somali and Teso, in addition to Swahili which is also featured in the national network.[20]

The importance of this emphasis given to the use of African languages in the media is that it reinforces the idea that information flow in the indigenous languages is a necessary requirement for mass involvement. To ignore them and concentrate on the use of official languages, such as English and French, in the media is not only to defeat the main aim of mass participation in development, but also to limit the advantages accruing from foreign industry and investment to a privileged urban elite, since 'most of the increase in wealth accrues to the local managerial and professional classes, who serve as junior partners to these foreign-owned firms'.[21] Besides, on the political front, it is the same elites who will be well placed to manipulate the apparatus of power.

The conclusion which seems inevitable given the situation of most developing countries is that a multilingual policy is the only viable avenue for development. Even Fishman, who had earlier associated Languages of Wider Communication (LWCs) with efficiency, now seems to see the drawback of a position that equates efficiency with monolingualism; for not only does he debunk the ludicrous idea that 'English improves the crops, raises the gross national product, avoids drought and earthquakes, and improves television', he now affirms that 'In a multilingual world it is obviously more efficient and rational to be multilingual than not' (Fishman, 1978: 45, 47). Foreign ideas, concepts and technology will undoubtedly be imported in a foreign language, but such concepts must be transmitted to the masses in the language that they can understand. The economic miracle achieved by countries such as Japan was not based on a widespread dissemination of English, rather it is the result of the indigenisation of such technology in Japanese, and the translation of the processes into terms that the ordinary factory hand can understand.

Patterns of Communication

Communication in the linguistic sense of verbal and non-verbal exchange is also crucial to the well-being and functioning of a state. Although it is usual to divide states into monolingual and multilingual, the fact is that there is no state in the world where language varieties do not occur. In multilingual states, bilinguals make language choice and are involved in both code-switching and code-mixing. In monolingual states, there are dialect as well as register varieties. It could be said, therefore, that language difference is an extreme form of language choice, the major difference being that in a monolingual situation, there is a standard (written or spoken) which is understood by all, while in a multilingual situation no such standard exists. One has to learn more than one language to be able to operate in more than one code.

Much has been made of linguistic heterogeneity as a barrier to communication, and there is a lot of truth in this. For example, a country may be multilingual, while a large number of individuals in it are not bilingual, and so communication becomes a problem. Similarly, there are bilinguals who use the languages they know in different domains, to the extent that for all practical purposes they are no better than monolinguals (Whiteley 1971: 122). In spite of all this, however, it is for reasons of basic survival that people have to get along in a multilingual situation. Typical situations include:

1. Learning the language of the immediate community in order to become integrated into the life of the community.

2. Learning a border language for trade purposes.

3. Learning a lingua franca, a Language of Wider Communication, or a national language for instrumental purposes.

Patterns of communication may range from simple non-verbal gestures to perfect coordinate bilingualism. In a comprehensive survey of non-verbal communication, Omondi (1979) has found that there is a definite pattern to gestures, just as there are to phonemes and their allophones. For example, just as there are similarities in beckoning for 'come', 'go' and signals for 'assent' and 'dissent', there are also differences in counting, for instance according to whether one starts with the thumb, or the index finger or the little finger. Some differences can lead to a breakdown in communication. The Bemba in Zambia and Luo in Kenya estimate the height of non-living things by a flat palm stretched out; for animate entities, however, the hand is cupped or held vertical. The Kikuyu of Kenya, on the other hand, do not make this distinction. There is, therefore, the possibility of a Luo misunderstanding a Kikuyu gesture as wishing a stunted growth for his child. What all this shows is that only a rudimentary kind of interchange can be effected through non-verbal communication.

It has also been shown that even where languages are not the same, some form of 'semi-communication' across languages is possible.[22] It would appear, however, that certain conditions are necessary in order for such communication to be possible. First, the languages must be very similar. The example of Nembe and Kalabari given by Wolff (1964) shows that the languages concerned are close enough to be dialects of the same language. Second, the degree of communication possible must be related to the degree of similarity between the languages. But even here there are sociolinguistic considerations that may interfere with ease of communication. As Wolff points out, linguistic similarity by itself is not a guarantee of interlingual communication. The classic example is that of the Nembe, who accept the similarity between their language and Kalabari and claim that they understand it. The Kalabari, on the other hand, consider themselves socio-economically superior and therefore disclaim any similarity between the two languages. In communication with the Nembe, they would rather speak Kalabari or pidgin. A similar situation is that of the Isoko and Okpe, who formerly identified themselves as Urhobo, claiming mutual intelligibility with other dialects of Urhobo; but, under political pressure for autonomy and ethnic identity, the Isoko have started claiming a distinctiveness that rules out mutual intelligibility with Okpe and other Urhobo dialects. Third, even when intelligibility is admitted, it must be noted that the type of haphazard communication that is possible between languages cannot sustain an elaborate exchange of information and may lead to frequent breakdown in communication.

Another pattern of communication is the contrast between horizontal and vertical communication. As Heine (1979) describes it, horizontal communication is typical of indigenous languages which are acquired spontaneously, freely learnt out of choice, associated with the masses, egalitarian and hence a symbol of solidarity, essentially oral and likely to become pidginized if used as a second language, and with which a speaker's performance is not subjected to normative evaluation. In contrast to this, vertical communication is typical of LWCs. They are learnt through formal teaching and, as a result of prescription or incentives, they are associated with the elites and hence their use implies prestige, authority and social distance; there being a long written tradition, there is strong pressure to conform to the norm and put strictures on deviations from the norm. In effect, a standard language exists as the norm, though dialectal variations are possible.

In general terms, the distinction drawn by Heine is valid; but in terms of its details, there are overgeneralizations that need to be qualified. For example, the elites and the masses often share the same indigenous language. That is why it is possible to talk of that language as a language of solidarity. Similarly, it may not be justified to conclude that the language of vertical communication is always a LWC. In a situation (for example in a rural area) where an African language is a lingua franca (e.g. Hausa, Swahili), that lingua franca assumes the role of a vertical language in relation to the other local languages which must be regarded as horizontal languages. Another departure from the pattern is the possibility of having two vertical languages. This is certainly the case in North Africa, where a LWC and classical Arabic are used in vertical communication.

Models of Communication

As in the case of dissemination of information through the media, communication in most African countries has to be approached from a multilingual angle, and perhaps the most feasible model is a *three-language model*: one or more languages at the local/regional, national, and international levels.

At the local level, there would be one or more in-group languages serving as a symbol of group solidarity. One of such languages may as well achieve greater prominence as a trade or regional language. The interplay of language acquisition and use in a multilingual setting has been well demonstrated by the study of the residents of Madina, a suburb of Accra, where over 80 languages are natively spoken by the residents and over 70% of the people claim a knowledge of three or more languages.[23] In a similar study of the Somolu area of Lagos, Scotton (1975) reports that only 5% of the 187 respondents speak no other language than their mother tongue, which is Yoruba. Forty-five per cent claim to speak two languages, 29% three, and 4% four languages. Three languages, English, Yoruba and pidgin, seem to be the norm for inter-ethnic communication, and few people can really get along with a knowledge of only one second language. In both these multilingual situations, the evidence shows that people are willing to learn another language to survive or become integrated. This is the basis for a multilingual model at the local/regional level – several local languages, but one regional language as a second language to the majority.

It is, of course, easier to postulate in theoretical terms that a particular language will take on the function of a regional language. When it comes to a decision on which language, problems are bound to arise. A scheme proposed for Nigeria by Nwoye (1978: 193) based on six zones illustrates this problem:

Language	*States*
Hausa	Kano, Gongola, Benue, Plateau, Kwara, Borno, Bauchi, Niger, Sokoto, Kaduna (*now* Kaduna and Katsina).
Igbo	Anambra, Imo
Yoruba	Lagos, Ogun, Ondo, Ọyọ
Efik	Cross River (*now* Cross River and Akwa Ibom)
Ijọ	Rivers
Edo	Bendel

While the largely monolingual states will have no difficulty in accepting the proposed languages, there will be problems in the multilingual states. For instance, how can Kwara, Borno, Benue and Plateau States accept Hausa as their state language? Even in Rivers and Cross River problems will arise. And Bendel State, which is a microcosm of Nigeria, cannot possibly operate with one regional language. What this points to is that a compromise may be required in some cases by which more than one regional or state language may be adopted as a transitional measure.

At the national level, there are very few countries which can adopt a monolingual model. Even in such countries as are monolingual, educational and technological considerations often lead to the adoption of an additional language, usually a LWC, as a transitional feature of national communication. But the sole use of a LWC as a means of communication at the national level effectively disfranchises a large section of the population and creates a gap between the masses and the elites. This point is not lost on African governments, since, in their general declarations of policy, they often stress the need for an indigenous means of national communication. The typical attitude is one of the following:

1. *To declare in favour of an African language and then do nothing about it (this can be called the Do-Nothing policy)*. A good example of this is Kenya's elaborately declaring Swahili as its national language while pursuing educational policies that favour English.

2. *To accept the idea of an African language in principle and opt for a natural evolution of one of the languages*. If purposefully implemented, this could be a positive step; but in many cases, the declaration is not matched by concrete implementation strategies. Thus, in effect, this sort of policy often amounts to the same thing as the Do-Nothing policy. Statements by highly-placed government functionaries, such as that it is 'necessary and desirable to continue to use [English] for our advancement in this nuclear and technological age until we are able to develop one or more of our native languages' or 'We have enough on our plate to keep us busy for a few years without having to worry about a common language',[24] tend to point to the ambivalence in attitude between intention and practice.

There are, of course, a few other governments that do not consider an indigenous medium of communication as a priority at all. Côte d'Ivoire is happy with French, and Senegal, in spite of its Wolof-speaking majority, also appears happy with French as a means of national communication. Cameroon, understandably a difficult case because of the absence of a dominant indigenous language, also appears to have settled for French and English. In the words of a former Cameroonian Minister, the African linguistic heritage

being so heterogeneous, so hopelessly fragmented, and none of these languages being the vehicle of science and technology, we are forced, for all our pride, to seek unity among ourselves, to seek modern development through alien tongues. And our ambition should be to give to those of our children who are able, the means to achieve great success in the use of these foreign languages, to possess over them the same mastery as their owners possess.[25]

In other words, the ultimate aim is native-like mastery of French and English by the young generation!

While a multilingual policy for national communication seems inevitable for most African countries, considerable advantage could be taken of natural bilingualism involving a major African lingua franca. This has been done in Tanzania with the spread of Swahili in urban areas, institutions, police and army barracks, and national service camps, where the language is reported to be the dominant language, and in rural areas, where it is often of equal status with the mother tongues.[26] A similar natural spread in the case of Wolof in Senegal, where even children born to non-Wolof speaking parents are becoming Wolof speakers, has a great potential for the development of an indigenous national language;[27] but the advantages and possibilities inherent in this situation have been largely neglected.

Communication at the international level is generally carried out by means of a LWC. Generally, this LWC is also the official language of communication at the national level. Although, because of the way colonial boundaries were drawn, peoples who speak the same language can be found in different countries, African languages spoken across national boundaries could be said to fall into two patterns:

1. *Languages predominantly spoken in one country but constituting a minority in other countries*
For example, Chichewa in Malawi compared with its minority status in Zambia and Mozambique; Ewe in Togo compared with its minority status in Ghana or Wolof in Senegal compared with its minority status in Gambia. In such cases, the question of international use of the common language does not arise.

2. *Languages predominantly spoken in more than one country*
For example, Somali in both Somalia and Djibouti, Swahili in Tanzania and Kenya, Hausa in Nigeria and Niger.[28] In principle, there is no reason why such languages cannot be used for communication between the countries concerned; but, in practice, the constraints are that the language in question also has to be the language of national communication in *both* countries, and there is also the protocol of diplomatic exchanges which have always been via a LWC.

For now, and in the foreseeable future, African languages are limited to trade contacts and the occasional goodwill gesture by a visiting Head of State speaking an African language (as, for example, when the Nigerian leader, General Ọbasanjọ, addressed an audience in Cotonou, Benin Republic in Yoruba in July 1978). The strong tradition of international communication through a LWC did not allow the now defunct East African Community of Tanzania, Kenya and Uganda to conduct its intergovernmental communication in Swahili, nor has it encouraged the Senegambia alliance of Senegal and Gambia to seek an alternative to communication through French and English.

The model of communication between African states has to be multilingual, since no single language is available as a means of inter-African communication. The Organization of African Unity (OAU) has three working languages, English, French and Arabic, and it has been the policy of the Organization to work towards the replacement of English and French with Swahili and Hausa. In fact, as part of the Organization's Language Plan of Action for Africa adopted by its Council of Ministers in Addis Ababa in July 1986, the Organization is enjoined to develop and promote the use of African languages with a view to bringing about the linguistic independence and identity of African nations.[29] Obviously, as long as those languages that the OAU intends to promote as international languages do not have the status of a national means of communication in member states, using them for communication at the international forum will be difficult, if not impossible.

The OAU is not the only organization interested in having African languages of international communication. A more radical proposal is that of the African Writers' Association, which has even advocated the adoption of Swahili as a Pan-African lingua franca. During the Festival of Black Arts and Culture (FESTAC) held in Lagos in 1977, a spokesman for the Association, the well-known Nigerian playwright and 1986 Nobel Laureate for Literature Wọle Ṣoyinka, repeated the call as a rallying point for African linguistic independence.[30]

Supporters of Swahili as a Pan-African lingua franca claim the following advantages for it:

1. It is already widely spoken by a sizeable population, particularly in Eastern and Central Africa.

2. It has been, and it is still being, used in several domains, including administration and education, with the consequent expansion of vocabulary.

3. There is already an appreciable volume of publications

in the language, including translations of works in English.

4. It is typologically similar to several Bantu/Bantoid languages in Africa.

5. It is non-tonal.

The major problem with the proposal to have Swahili as a Pan-African language is that there are large areas of Africa where Swahili is not spoken at all (for example, West Africa). This raises a number of issues: how will the language be implanted and spread to a reasonable segment of the population? how can the claims of Swahili be reconciled with those of internal languages being developed as a means of communication at regional or national levels? how will the priority of eradication of illiteracy through local languages fit in with the introduction of an external Pan-African medium? In any case, don't other languages have claims to the status of lingua franca, albeit for certain regions of the continent? For example, Hausa would appear to have a greater claim than Swahili as a means of communication for the West African region. The search for a single Pan-African language is probably one of the aspects of Africa's preoccupation with the number *one*. So far, no one has suggested that Africa should have only one leader. And if Black Africa does succeed in evolving a Pan-African language (a rather remote possibility), it will perhaps be the only continent in the world to have achieved such a feat![31] International communication in Africa is likely to continue to be on a multilingual model. If, at some point in the distant future, the role now performed by LWCs in this regard can be taken over by other languages, this could only be in terms of several languages, one for each region. One possibility would be Arabic for North Africa, Swahili for Central and Eastern Africa, Hausa for West Africa, and perhaps a Zulu-related language for Southern Africa.

One aspect that is often lost sight of is that there is no unanimity at all concerning the desirability of replacing LWCs as vehicles of international communication with African languages. While at the forum of the OAU countries are calling for this kind of innovation, a large number of member states also subscribe to Francophonie, a political and socio-economic movement whose aims are

> to strengthen the French language by maintaining a
> standard variety; to modernize its words through
> indigenization of English neologisms or the invention of

their own; to ensure that the language is used in all areas of communications, science, literature, interstate relations and organizations; and to remind or convince people of its noble qualities.[32]

Although ostensibly a reaction to the dominance of the English language on the international scene, Francophonie, with its requirement that the French language be used in all areas of communication and in interstate relations, runs counter to the aspirations of those advocating African regional languages of communication. It is a vivid reminder that the patterns of communication established in the colonial period are still very much with us and will probably continue to be for a long time to come.[33]

Notes to Chapter 2

1. See Fishman (1968b: 63).
2. See Unesco (1976a: 3-4).
3. See Lestage (1982: 8).
4. The countries listed include those that were not then independent, for example Namibia and overseas territories of some European countries. The literacy rates are also in respect of different years.
5. See Lestage (1982: 8).
6. See Adiseshiah (1976: 68-70).
7. See Unesco (1976a: 20).
8. See Campos (1980).
9. See Unesco (1987: 1-18).
10. See Rao (1966: 54; 97-110).
11. See Schumacher (1973: 190-1).
12. Excerpt from a talk given at the International Conference on Adult Education, Dar-es-Salaam, 21 June 1976, and reproduced as a Preface in Bataille (1976).
13. See Bataille (1976: 273-4).
14. Nieuwenhuijze (1982: 17-18, 54) has drawn attention to the dependency syndrome that tends to go with aid. The title of his book *Development Begins at Home* emphasizes the need for self-reliance.
15. See ACP-EEC Council of Ministers – Brussels (1985: 37).
16. See Schumacher (1973: 183-4).
17. The Mali experiment is reported in Dumont (1973).
18. See Unesco (1976a: 23-4).
19. The figures of books published refer to first editions only.
20. See Unesco (1975).
21. See Safa (1974: 376).
22. The term 'semi-communication' is used by Haugen (1966a) to refer to communication across language boundaries as in the case of Scandinavian languages.

23. For a description of the Madina study, see Berry (1971).
24. The first quotation is from the speech made to Parliament by the Nigerian Minister of Education (Federation of Nigeria 1961-2), and the second by the Deputy Minister of Education for Ghana (Agyei, n.d.).
25. See Fonlon (1975: 204).
26. See Abdulaziz (1971).
27. See Calvet and Wioland (1967).
28. For a list of African languages spoken across national boundaries, see Unesco (1979).
29. See OAU (1986).
30. See Ṣoyinka (1977).
31. By comparison, the European Community, comprising twelve countries, makes use of nine languages in conducting its business – this in spite of the cultural homogeneity of its peoples.
32. See Weinstein (1983: 167).
33. See Bamgboṣe (1979).

3

Language and Education

Multilingualism and Education

The importance of education in the context of a developing country seems too obvious to require any elaboration. As was pointed out in the discussion of national development in Chapter Two, literacy is crucial to mass participation; but since literacy itself is only a part of education, the crux of the contribution of education lies in the entire spectrum ranging from literacy to higher education. Education is, therefore, not only the basis of mass participation, it is a means of upward social mobility, manpower training, and development in its widest sense of the full realization of human potential and the utilization of this potential and the nation's resources for the benefit of all.

Options in Language Education

In talking about education, it is inevitable that the question of language should arise, since it is mainly through language that knowledge is transmitted. Three major questions are involved in the role of language in education: what language? for which purpose? and at which level?[1]

The question of what language to use in education is a problematic one in any multilingual country, particularly one that has also been subjected to the inevitable imposition of a foreign official language arising from colonialism. First, there is the child's mother tongue, which is the medium of informal education in the home and of socialization processes among his peer group. Second, particularly in the case of speakers of minority languages, there is the language of the immediate community which serves as a local or regional lingua franca and is, therefore, mastered by the child. Third, as an alternative to a language of the immediate community, there is, in some African countries, a widely-spoken lingua franca or national language. Fourth, there is a Language of Wider Communication which was also the official language during the colonial period, and which has become a second language in the countries concerned. Fifth, there is a language associated with religion (for example, Classical Arabic in several African countries with Muslim populations).[2] Sixth, there is a LWC learnt as a foreign language.

Each of the six types of languages has a claim to be used in the educational process. Examples of such uses are the mother tongue in primary education in many African countries such as Ghana, Nigeria and Uganda, a language of the immediate community used in teaching many children in Zambia, the national language (Swahili) as a medium of primary education in Tanzania, and an official LWC at some level of education in all African countries, Arabic in Nigeria and English in Senegal.

Language may be used for three purposes in education: literacy, subject, and medium of instruction. Literacy, in this connection, is taken to refer either to initial literacy for children being introduced to the rudiments of reading and writing or to adults also being trained to read and write.[3] A language may be taught as a subject without any implication of its further use as a medium of instruction, but whenever a language is used as a medium of instruction, the implication is that it is also taught as a subject.

The third question concerns when a language is introduced; and this is often associated with levels of education: primary, secondary, and post-secondary. A language may be introduced as a subject at any point at each of the three levels; but for a language to serve as a medium of instruction at secondary and higher levels, it would have to have been taught as a subject at the primary level. It is possible for one medium to give way to another, as when a mother tongue medium is replaced by a LWC medium. It is also possible for two media of instruction to be used concurrently, as when some subjects are taught through one medium and others are taught through another medium. For obvious reasons, introduction of literacy skills involves only the initial level of primary education or adult literacy. The term 'mother tongue education' is used in this book to refer to the use of an indigenous language in education for any purpose and at any level.

Of the six types of languages, two types are clearly very restricted in their scope. The first is a language of religion which can function only as a subject, perhaps at all levels of education. The second is a foreign LWC which can also only be a subject of secondary or higher level of education. In fact, because of the poor teaching of foreign languages in many African schools and the problem of availability of teachers, the time may yet come when such teaching is restricted to the post-secondary level. We are now left with four types of languages, two of which are alternatives.

Based on the questions 'what language?' and 'for which purpose?' it is possible to arrive at nine possibilities. To these may be added the further qualification of time of introduction of the language in respect of its being taught as a subject or as a medium of instruction. The nine possibilities may be shown as in Table 3.1.

1. *Mother tongue for literacy.* This is the most wide-spread practice in adult literacy, even in the countries that do not have mother tongue education at any level in the formal school system. There is, however, considerable difference in terms of initial literacy. In situations where mother tongue education is practised at the primary school level, initial literacy is generally through the mother tongue. However, where the practice is to start education through a LWC, initial literacy is usually done through the LWC after a period of oral introduction of the language.

2. *Mother tongue as a subject.* This is always the practice in a situation where the mother tongue is also used as a medium of instruction. It is, of course, also possible to teach the mother tongue purely as a subject. This frequently happens in higher education, where Departments of Linguistics and Languages offer courses even up to higher degree level in African languages. A mother tongue is not usually offered as a subject at secondary level if it has not been taught at primary level.

3. *Mother tongue as a medium.* This is largely restricted to those countries that have a mother tongue education policy, particularly at primary level. Variations are possible, as in those cases where certain so-called easy subjects, such as Nature Study or Story-telling are taught in a mother tongue, while more difficult subjects such as Arithmetic and Geography are taught in a LWC. The use of an African mother tongue as a medium of instruction beyond primary level is rare. Somali is one such example.

Table 3.1. Language type and function in education

	Literacy	*Subject*	*Medium*
Mother tongue	×	×	×
Comm./Nat. Lang.	×	×	×
LWC	×	×	×

4. *Community or National Language for literacy.* This involves the use of a language other than the child's mother tongue for initial literacy. The extent to which the approach can succeed depends on the mastery of the language by the pupils concerned. Where children already speak the language well, initial literacy can easily be conducted in it with almost the same facility as in a mother tongue; but where children or adults do not already speak the language, initial literacy is bound to present a problem as learners cope with the learning of a new sound system at the same time as they learn to represent such sounds through symbols on paper.

5. *Community or National Language as a subject.* This is a feasible practice and can be an alternative to subjecting children to initial literacy in a language other than their mother tongue. Provided the language is not introduced too early in the school course and there is sufficient motivation to acquire it (for instance, because of its instrumental value), this practice is likely to yield good results. In Kenya, where Swahili is the national language, the medium of instruction in primary schools is still English, but provision is made for the teaching of Swahili as a subject. But problems are likely to occur when the teacher is not proficient in the approved language. Experience with such practice in Zambia, for instance, has shown that all sorts of deviation from the expected norm are possible. For example, the teacher may use his own mother tongue in preference to the approved language; he may teach another subject during the period allotted to language; he may leave the children to read on their own; or he may use English or another language while pretending to teach the approved language. Another source of

difficulty may be linguistic heterogeneity in the composition
of school or class populations, with the result that while
some children already possess a good mastery of the
approved language because it is their mother tongue, others
are grappling with the problem of mastering it because it is
a new language.[4]

6. *Community Language or National Language as a
medium.* This is only practicable where the language in
question is already widely spoken in the country. Even so,
problems may arise where there are differences in exposure
to the language. For example, in Tanzania, where Swahili
is used as a medium of instruction in primary schools,
there are four distinct categories of children for whom the
practice has different implications: a minority of native
speakers, a large majority of second language speakers,
speakers of Bantu languages like Swahili, and speakers of
non-Bantu languages.[5] One of the challenges of a policy of
using a Community or National Language as a medium is
to ensure through intensive early or remedial teaching that
disparities in mastery are, as far as possible, minimized if
not entirely eliminated.

7. *LWC for literacy.* The theory behind this practice is
that, given an initial exposure to oral/aural training in a
LWC, the children's mother tongue can be ignored while
the rudiments of reading and writing can be effectively
taught through the LWC. The question is not so much
whether this can be done, but at what cost. Given sufficient
time, any child can learn any sounds and also learn to
associate them with appropriate symbols in writing; what
needs to be explained in this approach, however, is why an
asset already possessed by the child should be ignored.
Literacy through the mother tongue or any other language
that the child already speaks means that he will not be
grappling with two difficulties at the same time, that is,
learning a new sound system and learning to represent
such sounds in writing. Using the sound system of the
child's language for teaching literacy means that he will
only be concerned with how to reduce the sounds he already
knows to writing; and once he has learnt to write such
sounds, this should facilitate his writing of any other
sounds that are similar.

8. *LWC as a subject*. Since, for most African countries, a LWC is bound to be used at some point as the medium of instruction, the use of a LWC as a subject only is normally associated with the lower classes of primary school prior to a change-over to an English medium at the upper primary level, or all classes at primary level, where an African language serves as a medium of instruction for the entire primary education. In the few countries where an African language or Arabic is used as a medium of instruction beyond primary education (e.g. Somali in Somalia, Arabic in Sudan), a LWC may be taught as a subject beyond the primary level.

9. *LWC as a medium*. This is the typical practice for most African countries. The LWC may be used as a medium from the first class of primary school (as in practically all the so-called French-speaking African countries and in some other countries such as Sierra Leone, Zambia and Kenya); it may be introduced as a medium at some point during the primary school course (as in Ghana, Nigeria, Uganda); and it may become a medium at secondary level (as in Tanzania). No matter at which point a LWC becomes a medium of instruction, it continues from there until the highest levels of education. It should be noted, however, that the practice of a LWC medium is often different from the theory. For example, in many situations where a LWC is supposed to be a medium in early primary education, a mother tongue or a community language is often used instead.[6]

Given the three types of languages which we can now label as L_1 (Mother tongue), L_2 (Community Language or National Language) and L_3 (Language of Wider Communication), there are several options possible in terms of combinations of use at the primary school level for initial literacy, subject and medium of instruction. Although in theory there are twenty-seven possible combinations, the actually occurring options are restricted because of the following conditions:

1. If a language is a medium of instruction, it is automatically a subject.

2. If L_1 or L_2 is a medium of instruction, initial literacy must have been in L_1 or L_2 respectively.

3. If L_2 is a medium of instruction, L_1 can only be a subject and vice versa.

4. If L_3 is used for initial literacy, it must also be used as a medium of instruction.

5. In all cases, L_3 must be either a subject or a medium of instruction.

The resulting options are:

1. L_3 for initial literacy and as a medium of instruction, for instance French in Côte d'Ivoire and Senegal.

2. L_1 for initial literacy and L_3 as a medium of instruction, for instance several minority languages for initial literacy and English as a medium in Nigeria.

3. L_1 for initial literacy and subject, L_3 as a medium of instruction, for instance minority languages with an existing script, e.g. Iṣẹkiri for initial literacy and subject, and English as a medium, in Nigeria.

4. L_1 for initial literacy, L_1 and L_3 as media of instruction, as for instance in Ghana, Uganda, Nigeria. Variations of this option include L_1 and L_3 as consecutive media of instruction involving the use of L_1 as a medium of instruction for some years (usually three) followed by English as a medium; and complementary media of instruction involving the teaching of some subjects in L_1 and others in English. For example, in Uganda, the English medium is progressively introduced, beginning with Mathematics and Physical Education in the fourth year, extending to Science, Geography, Art, Crafts and Music in the fifth year and all subjects in the sixth and seventh years.[7]

5. L_1 for initial literacy and as a medium of instruction; L_3 as a subject, for instance Somali and English respectively in Somalia.

6. L_1 and L_2 as subject, L_3 for initial literacy and as a medium of instruction, as for instance in Kenya, where the L_2 is Swahili and L_3 is English.

7. L_1 or L_2 as a subject, L_3 for initial literacy and as a medium of instruction, as for instance in Zambia, where there are seven approved Zambian languages taught as a subject which may or may not be the child's mother tongue, and English is the L_3.

8. L_2 for initial literacy and as a medium of instruction, L_3 as a subject, for instance Swahili and English respectively in Tanzania. For the minority of children for whom Swahili is a L_1, the option is the same as in (4) above.

9. L_2 for initial literacy, L_2 and L_3 as media of instruction, for instance Hausa in parts of Plateau State of Nigeria taught as a community language for initial literacy and used with English as a medium.

10. L_2 for initial literacy and as subject; L_3 as a medium. (No example found, but a theoretical possibility.)

In addition to the above options, it must be noted that in those countries where Arabic is not a national or official language but has to be taught in schools for religious reasons, it could be combined with an existing option as a subject. For example, in Northern and Western Nigeria, there are schools that combine option (3) with Arabic as a subject.

Constraints in Language Education

Although in the discussion of options the possible choices have been presented as if they are free choices, there are, in fact, external constraints that determine particular choices made by given countries. The most important of such constraints are historical, sociolinguistic, sociocultural, economic, theoretical, pedagogic and political.[8]

Language in education provides the best illustration of what has come to be known as *an inheritance situation*: how the colonial experience continues to shape and define post-colonial problems and practices.[9] Thus, while it would seem that African nations make policy in education, what they actually do is carry on the logic of the policies of the past. Nowhere is this more in evidence than in the very languages selected, the roles assigned to them, the level at which languages are introduced and the difficulty of changing any of these.

Throughout Africa the language of education includes a colonial language which is a LWC. Thus, all former British colonies have English, all former French and Belgian colonies have French, all former Portuguese colonies have Portuguese and the only former Spanish colony has Spanish. In Cameroon, where the western part was a former British colony and the eastern part a French colony, English and French are both languages of education. In addition, those countries subjected to Arabic influence leading to the establishment of Islam also tend to have Arabic as a school subject (e.g. Nigeria) or as a medium of instruction, if Arabic is also an official language of the country (e.g. Mauritania, Sudan).

The use or non-use of African languages in education is also

largely a function of the colonial heritage. African countries
divide neatly into two groups which reflect the colonial practices.
Mother tongue education is not practised in the former French
and Portuguese colonies, and this is simply a survival of their
colonial policy of assimilation which encouraged their own
languages and discouraged African languages. Mother tongue
education is practised in the former British colonies (with the
exception of Sierra Leone), and this is in accordance with the
educational policy of the British which encouraged mother
tongue education in British territories. Although the Belgians
also encouraged the teaching of African languages in their
former colony of the Congo, the country now known as Zaire
has abandoned this colonial policy and opted for education
through French.

Where mother tongue education was practised, its role was
limited to initial literacy, a medium of instruction at the lower
classes of the primary school, and/or a subject at primary and
higher levels. Adult literacy was also typically conducted in an
African language. This is precisely the prevalent situation in
Africa today. The colonial role of African languages persists as
does the role of the colonial LWC as a medium of instruction
from upper primary or secondary to higher levels of education.
Thus, not only has the function of each type of language
survived, so has the level at which it is introduced. African
languages as media of instruction are restricted to lower levels
of education, typically the primary school, and LWCs are
reserved for higher levels.

In spite of about thirty years of independence for most
African states, the difficulty of breaking away from the
established historical patterns indicates the persistence of the
inheritance situation. Since the colonial practice gave pride of
place to the colonial language, breaking away should mean
according a greater role to indigenous languages. This has been
the subject of experiments or plans in some African countries,
and the outcome has been one of the following:

1. *Expansion in the use of an African language as a
medium of instruction to the entire primary school course
and even beyond.* For example, the use of Somali as a
medium of instruction up to secondary level or the use of
Swahili as a medium of instruction throughout primary
education. But even here, the problem of breaking away
from the past is obvious. The original plan, when Swahili

became a medium of instruction at primary level in Tanzania in 1967, was to extend the use of Swahili as a medium of instruction to secondary education. Not only has this plan not materialized, the Tanzanian Minister for National Education was quoted in 1986 as saying that English would continue to be a medium of instruction in secondary schools for a long time to come.[10]

2. *Experimentation without the necessary policy back-up.* For example, attempts to use Wolof in initial literacy in Senegal, mother tongue education in some Cameroonian and Sierra Leonean languages, and the use of Yoruba as a medium of instruction for primary education in the Six-Year Project in Nigeria.

The reverse development of moving away from mother tongue education to an increasing role for a LWC appears to be a much easier practice. Although, superficially, it looks like a departure from the colonial tradition, in actual fact it is a reinforcement of that tradition, in that it gives greater prominence to the former colonial language. It is also much easier to accomplish, as can be seen in the number of countries that have tried it at one point or another: Zaire moving exclusively to French as a medium of instruction, Kenya and Zambia to English and, at certain points in their language educational history, Ghana and Northern Nigeria opting for the so-called 'Straight-for-English' policy.

The overall effect of historical constraint is that African countries remain prisoners of the past. The established practices are so overwhelming that it becomes virtually impossible to break away from them. When the role of the LWC as a language of science and technology is added to the picture, historical constraint is further reinforced by the argument that a language that is going to be needed in any case for higher education, science and technology might as well begin to feature in the educational process as soon as possible.

The sociolinguistic constraint concerns language status, size of speakers, and state of language development. In any multilingual situation, the fact of multiplicity of language implies a choice, and the assignment of different roles to languages depending on a number of factors. Some languages are regarded as official, national, regional, community, or local. No matter how defined, a language accorded the status of a national or official language must have a prominent place in education much higher than the role given to other languages. Similarly, depending on the situation in a country, a regional or community language may also be given a role as a subject or even, in some cases, as a medium of instruction.

The size of the population speaking each language is also an important factor in the assignment of roles. Other things being equal, a language spoken by ten million people is likely to have a greater role in education than one spoken by half a million people. This is because, for such a language, a ready pool of pupils and potential teachers is easily available and materials can be provided on a more economical scale. This, however, should not be taken to mean that minority languages are to be ignored. It only means that the roles for major and minority languages will be different. While a programme of full mother tongue medium for the entire primary education may be viable for a major language, it is certainly less so for a minority language for which the only possible role may be simply use in initial literacy or as a medium of instruction in the lower classes of the primary school. Related to the problem of size is the linguistic composition of school populations. This is particularly significant in urban areas where the incidence of mixed classes has often impeded mother tongue education.

No matter how large the population of speakers of a language is, it is only when the language has been reduced to writing and materials made available in it that it can be used in education. Hence, a major factor in the selection of language for any role whatever is the state of development of the language. A language with a long literary tradition has an advantage over one that does not. A good example of this is the Efik-Ibibio language cluster in Nigeria for which the early missionaries reduced Efik to writing and produced language and literary materials. Although in terms of numbers Ibibio is the major language of the cluster, the early tradition of writing put Efik at an advantage and made it the variety used for initial literacy and medium of instruction in lower primary classes. In the absence of a written tradition, a decision to use a language in education will at the same time involve deliberate language planning activities including devising of an orthography, production of primers and other reading materials, training of teachers, etc. As these take time and also involve financial costs, quite often such a language remains excluded from the educational process. Another aspect of language development is the need to evolve adequate terminology for teaching school subjects. This will have to be done if African languages are to be used as media of instruction.

The sociocultural constraint is usually linked with the desire to ensure that a people's culture which a language represents is not ignored in the educational process. Translated into educational policy, it means that at some point in the course of a child's education, he must have an opportunity of learning his language or learning in it. As this factor is often pitched against that of cost and the need for technological development, it is sometimes suggested that a nation faces 'an unpleasant choice between the need for economic development and the desire for cultural survival'. Furthermore, it is suggested that while a nation may be concerned with preserving a culture through its language, the interest of the child in terms of an effective education to fit him for the modern world may be the exact opposite of this concern. Thus, the question boils down to whether one wants to save the language or save the child.[11] Considerations such as these reduce the importance of the sociocultural constraint in that the argument shifts from the desirability of a cultural component to the superiority of education through a LWC. It is doubtful, however, whether there is really any need for a dichotomy here. There is no reason why the introduction of a cultural component cannot take several forms, the most minimal of which is provision for teaching a language as a subject and the most considerable of which is using it as a medium of instruction. How this is done and for how long will depend on the language in question.

If the cultural component is taken as a variable, the sociocultural constraint can be presented in terms of the goals envisaged for a bilingual education programme. According to the classificatory scheme proposed by Siguán and Mackey (1987: 48-9), such goals are associated with different options ranging from non-use of the first language to a maximum use of it. Clearly, non-use is a negation of the cultural input and so will not qualify to be included here. But other goals and options are relevant: use of L_1 as a subject only corresponds to recognition of linguistic and cultural plurality; equal use of both L_1 and L_2 as media indicates a concern for bilingualism and biculturalism; combination of a L1 as a medium with a minority language as a subject or medium is an appeal to cultural harmony and coexistence; use of L_1 as a medium with L_3 as a subject is designed to widen the student's cultural horizon; use of L_1 as a medium giving way to L_3 emphasizes cultural enrichment through a broadening of knowledge to include that available in a LWC; and equal use of L_1 and L_3 as media focuses attention on international understanding and solidarity.[12] The attraction of this sort of scheme is that it widens the scope of the cultural component of a language education to include not just the native culture, which supporters of mother tongue education tend to focus on, but cultures associated with all the languages used in the educational system.

The economic constraint is related to the multiplicity of languages and the excessive cost of providing education in all of them. The strong version of the constraint is that there are far too many languages and many of them lack a written literature. To provide written materials in all of them is a practical impossibility; hence, any question of using all languages for education does not arise. Modern education requires instruction *not* in more and more languages but in the most effective language possible. Consequently, many of the world's minority languages are doomed to extinction.[13] The weak version of the constraint is that advances in linguistics and printing technology have made mass production of materials in thousands of languages possible; therefore it is possible to use all of the world's languages at all levels of education. But what would be the point of this? Is the amount of investment justified considering that many of these languages are 'unproductive'? A language is like a currency: the more it can buy, the greater value it has. Consequently, a LWC which is of wider currency and can give the child access to modern education and technology and ensure for the nation rapid economic development is obviously to be preferred.[14]

Both the strong and weak versions of the economic constraint exaggerate the real intention of mother tongue education. No one has claimed that it is possible to use *all languages* as vehicles of education *at all levels*! Rather, the claim is that varying degrees of mother tongue education are possible, ranging from adult literacy or initial literacy to medium of instruction; and the continuing need for a LWC is emphasized. But if one must go by the strictly economic argument, the real cost of education in a LWC must be quantified in terms of such factors as poor performance, drop-out rate, cost of recruitment of foreign personnel and the use of material ill-adapted to the local situation.[15]

The economic argument when used against mother tongue education tends to ignore the important role of education in development which should be concerned with the liberation of the human potential for the welfare of the community. As some commentators have observed, existing school systems in Third World countries 'have served only to train tiny élites to run a bureaucracy and the modern sector of an economy while neglecting the training of human resources capable of stimulating production in areas essential to the welfare of the majority of the population'.[16] For this situation to change, grass-roots education will be needed, and the use of several indigenous languages in such education would seem to be inevitable.

Although bilingualism is a natural phenomenon in most multilingual countries, when it comes to deciding on the language of education, the arguments advanced often ignore this fact as choices are presented in terms of either one or the other. A major constraint in the choice of language in education has been the theoretical one based on the problems of learning and cognitive development. Questions are raised about the psychology of the child as he tries to cope with new experiences in the learning process. Is he likely to learn faster and better using his own language or using a language foreign to him? Will his cognitive development be affected positively or negatively? Will his personality be affected?[17]

One of the earliest pronouncements on this matter which was to influence educational practice in many developing countries was the recommendation of the Unesco Meeting of Experts (which took place in Paris in 1951 and produced its report in 1953), as follows:

> On educational grounds, we recommend that the use of the mother tongue be extended to as late a stage in education as possible. In particular, pupils should begin their schooling through the medium of the mother-tongue, because they understand it best and because to begin their school life in the mother tongue will make the break between home and the school as small as possible.[18]

This recommendation reinforced the practice of early mother tongue education in several countries and was used to support its introduction where it did not formerly exist.

Although the recommendation is backed by the famous Iloilo experiment in the Philippines, which examined the relative effectiveness of using Hiligaynon as opposed to English as a medium of instruction, it has often been attacked as a mere declaration not based on any objective evidence. The Iloilo experiment itself, which came to the conclusion that the experimental group taught in the mother tongue performed better than the control group and even caught up with them in English within only six months of being exposed to English, was subjected to criticism on the grounds of inadequacy of tests, non-isolation of variables, unequal curricula, teacher competence, drop-out rate, etc.[19] In fact, a subsequent study (the Rizal study), designed to find out the most appropriate time to introduce reading in English, came to the opposite conclusion, that those who used English longest had the highest scores in the sixth grade.

The controversy about which medium offers the best chance of learning for the child has led to the mounting of different experiments. In Africa, there was the Iganga experiment in Uganda in which two classes were taught Geography, one in English and the other in a mother tongue, with the result that the class taught in English performed better.[20] In Kenya, there was the work of the Special Centre which in 1958 embarked on a pilot project of using English as the medium of instruction in some primary schools for Asian children. The success of the project led to its extension to other schools in 1961, thus reversing the long-standing practice of mother tongue education in the first three years of primary education.[21]

The claim that the earlier the teaching of English is begun the better it is for the child was to have a profound influence on the educational language policy of a few African countries. Apart from Kenya, Zambia also adopted the policy; and even the then administration of Northern Nigeria opted for the 'Straight-for-English' policy. Earlier, Ghana, on attainment of independence in 1957, had opted for the English medium policy.[22] The change of policy from a mother tongue medium to an English medium in some of the countries concerned is further reinforced by the interest of foreign donors in the spread of the teaching of English, which they most willingly supported through the donation of teaching materials, training of teachers, and supply of expatriate teachers and consultants.

The Six Year Primary Project in Nigeria (which will be

discussed in full later in this chapter) was started in 1970, and came to the conclusion that teaching through the mother tongue facilitated more meaningful learning than teaching through English.

Outside Africa, the most famous experiment in bilingual education was the St Lambert experiment in Montreal in Canada, in which English-speaking children were taught in French from the first class of primary school, with only a short period allotted to English language skills. In the upper classes, 60% of the instruction was in French and 40% in English. The project, begun in 1965, came to the conclusion that learning through a second language was feasible and did not lead to any psychological handicap, since children in the experimental class still identified with English Canadian values.[23] Variations in the original experiment, now known as the 'early total immersion' programme (since it involves the use of French as a medium from the first day at school), have since been tried out. These include 'early partial immersion', involving an alternate use of French and English in each year of schooling, and 'late immersion', involving the use of French as a medium in the upper classes. Varying degrees of success are reported for immersion programmes, with the early immersion programme having an edge over the others.[24]

Because of the conflicting results from experiments in bilingual education, it is often believed either that one practice is as good as another or that a practice that has been shown to succeed in one situation ought to succeed in another. For instance, if making English-speaking children learn in French from their first day at school can succeed in Canada, why should not Ugandan children have total early immersion in English? The answer to this question is that results which are valid for a given situation cannot be generalized to cover other situations, for the following reasons:

1. There is a problem concerning the assumptions made in the use of terms such as 'reading' and 'transfer'. For instance, to say that, in a certain experiment, X group reads better than Y group may be no more than to claim that the group in question is able to decode symbols with little understanding. Similarly, a test of transfer of skills may ignore the complex nature of the processes involved, with the result that it could be administered at an inappropriate stage leading to unreliable results.[25]

2. A certain element of bias can hardly be ruled out as most bilingual education experiments start with some hypothesis which the investigators are trying to prove or disprove. For instance, in the context of a policy that favours assimilation through the spread of a LWC, results showing its superiority are often obtained, while in the context of a policy that favours cultural authenticity and pluralism, a mother tongue medium is likely to be shown as producing better results. The bias of investigators is sometimes betrayed in the underlying assumptions of the experiment, the questions posed, and the way the results are reported.

3. There are considerable differences in experiments which can be related to differences in the quality of programmes. Such possible differences include the materials used, the curriculum, teacher quality and adequacy, and methodology. Comparing programmes without an awareness of these variables may lead to a false attribution of the success or failure of an experiment to the medium.[26]

4. Bilingual experiments are never conducted in a vacuum. The sociocultural setting often determines what sort of pupils get into the programme, their attitudes as well as those of their parents, and their motivation. For instance, in those studies that show that pupils do as well as native speakers when taught through a foreign language, the children concerned come from upper- or middle-class homes, whereas studies that support mother tongue education tend to involve children from subordinate groups or non-dominant languages. To generalize from one situation to the other is to ignore the vital sociocultural difference.[27]

Earlier experiments in bilingual education appear to have been designed to answer the question: should there or should there not be education in more than one language? If not, which is the better language in which to provide education? Today, the attitude towards bilingual education is more positive, and the question seems to have shifted to timing rather than the principle of bilingual education. In the African context, this should mean a recognition that there should be a role for indigenous languages in education as well as for LWCs. That this lesson is yet to find a translation into policy is probably a result of the inertia of changing existing practices.

The pedagogic constraint concerns the conditions and facilities for teaching languages; and the crucial factor in this connection is the teacher problem. Any educational language policy requires for its effectiveness the availability of teachers. In the case of mother tongue education, such teachers must either be native speakers or have considerable competence in the language or languages they are required to teach. For major languages, perhaps this will not be a serious problem; but for minority languages, it could be a major constraint. Even when there are enough teachers to teach a particular language, the policy of deployment of teachers may create problems. For example, in Zambia, there is a policy of appointing teachers to teach in regions other than their own. The outcome of this is that many teachers find themselves in areas where they are unable to teach the approved language of the region.[28]

Another source of difficulty is the question of training. In many African countries, a large number of primary school teachers are either untrained or have received only minimal training. In particular, methodology for first language teaching is often neglected, the assumption being that if one can speak the language, one should be able to teach it. The result of this is that mother tongue education is often carried out in a perfunctory manner. Although the methodology of teaching LWCs tends to be taken more seriously, the same problem of inadequacy may arise, since every primary school teacher is supposed to be a good model for imitation by pupils learning languages such as English and French. As we shall see later in this chapter, this assumption contributes to the poor performance of pupils in these languages as well as in the other subjects for which they are used as media of instruction.

The political constraint manifests itself in several ways. First, there is a general attitude by governments that language policy matters are sensitive. As has rightly been observed, 'being typically cumbersome and conservative, educational systems usually prefer incremental changes by trial and error that do not unduly unsettle the status quo'.[29] Hence, there is a reluctance to change existing policies, particularly in the direction of increased mother tongue education. That is why only a few countries in Africa, such as Tanzania and Somalia, have succeeded in moving in this direction. Second, even when there is pressure to change, for example, to emphasize mother tongue education as an aspect of authenticity and cultural renewal, governments generally find it more convenient to pay lip-service to such goals and then quietly carry on with a LWC medium. For example, in spite of a resolution adopted in 1976 by African Ministers of Education to the effect that the requirements of authenticity and modernity in education dictate that national languages must be restored as languages of instruction and as vehicles of scientific and technical progress,[30] the educational practice of most African nations has remained unchanged in respect of the language of education. All that one hears is that plans are being made to make changes, but no progress is made beyond such pronouncements. Third, the attitude of those in power can influence both policy and how it is implemented. For example, the inclusion of Nzema as one of Ghana's nine approved languages is justified on the grounds that it is one of the languages spoken across the national boundary (i.e. in Côte d'Ivoire). In reality, the choice probably had much more to do with the fact that it was the native language of the then President, Dr Kwame Nkrumah. Similar cases of intervention include President Senghor's vigorous views on Wolof orthography in Senegal, President Banda's virtual veto power on vocabulary innovations in Chichewa in Malawi, and the reported rejection of a grammar of Kabiye by President Eyadema of Togo on the grounds that it was not based on his own dialect.[31]

Mother Tongue in Primary Education

The advantages of a good mastery of a LWC and a prominent role for it in the educational system in Africa seem too obvious to require any special pleading. As long as science and technology are transmitted in these languages, an almost unchangeable role is assured for them as media of instruction in secondary and tertiary levels of education. With the advances in recent years in computer technology, a great deal of learning and processing of knowledge now has to take place through the use of these machines, and, as is well known, computer language is based largely on LWCs and other European languages, but not on any African language.[32]

Recognition of the importance of a LWC and an insistence that it should oust African languages altogether as a medium of instruction are two different things. It is all too easy in overstating the case for LWCs to come to such a conclusion.

Slogans such as 'earlier means better' or 'longer means better' are used to justify this position[33] and reflected in views such as the following:

> . . . the mastery of a second or foreign language to the point it can be used professionally takes time. That is why the study of foreign languages is, where possible, being introduced into lower and lower grades of the curriculum. The better one knows how to use the language, the sooner one can use what is available in it.[34]

Contrary to expectation, long periods of English teaching have often not resulted in greater mastery. In a test of competence, administered together with a questionnaire, to selected schools in Uganda, it was found that, in spite of concentration on English teaching and its use as a medium of instruction, no significant differences were recorded between reading competence in English and in an indigenous language. In fact, the entire study showed that the teacher factor was more important than length of English teaching or even materials.[35] The reason for this sort of outcome is not far to seek. The practice of teaching English at primary school level rests on the assumption that all primary school teachers can teach English effectively. Unfortunately, since a large proportion of such teachers are untrained, they not only teach English badly but provide a poor model for their pupils to imitate. The result is that at the end of a long course of instruction in English, the level of competence attained is still quite poor.[36] Besides, the fact that children whose knowledge of English is inadequate have to cope with learning other subjects in English means equally poor performance in these subjects as well, and frequently high repeat and drop-out rates.

The unsatisfactory results from English language teaching at primary school level may be seen as a negative justification for the alternative approach, which favours mother tongue medium at least in the earlier years of primary education. There is, in fact, a positive justification, for which there is a strong version and a weak version. The strong version usually appeals to the need for preservation of a people's cultural heritage[37] and the fundamental human right to 'the use of the mother tongue in the initial phase of school life'.[38] But the kind of right that the strong version espouses is sometimes redefined by critics to include not only the right for languages to exist but also to choose not to exist:

Languages have the right to live, but for the sake of
larger unity they must give way to others for official
functions. Languages have the right to die and to retreat
from the public domain; and individuals who demand
scarce resources to publish, teach, and revive all
languages in the name of human rights threaten the
cohesion of the national community, the ultimate
guarantor of those rights.[39]

Although the opposition of sectional and national rights
implicit in the attack on the strong version is an exaggeration,
it must be accepted that basing language use in education on
human rights will virtually make choice impossible. In areas of
extreme linguistic fragmentation and in certain urban centres
characterized by linguistic heterogeneity, there may be no
alternative to the use of a community language or even a LWC
as a compromise medium of instruction. Similarly, some
minority languages may have to be employed only for initial
literacy and then abandoned because the school populations
involved do not make their use as media of instruction viable.
These are already violations of a human rights conception of
language in education.

The weak version of the positive justification for the use of
the mother tongue in the early years of primary education is
that by the time a child enrols in a primary school at the age of
six, he would have developed a capacity to use one language or
the other, in most cases his home language or mother tongue or
the language of the immediate community. Learning through
such a language will provide a smooth transition from the world
of the home to the world of the school. In any case, a situation
in which a child has to cope with a new system of sounds in a
language while at the same time learning to represent such
sounds as written symbols is most undesirable. Initial literacy
should, therefore, be conducted in a language that the child
already knows and, depending on other factors such as state of
development of the language, size of speakers and teacher
availability, this language should continue to be used as a
medium of instruction for as long as possible in primary
education. This version of justification for mother tongue
education makes possible a flexible approach in that it allows a
variety of practices depending on the situation.

There is ample evidence that the idea of bilingual education is becoming more and more attractive as an option to the hitherto monolingual education policy through a LWC. For example, the Ford Foundation, whose earlier concern was for the improvement of English Language teaching, has shifted from this narrow concern to a more comprehensive language improvement effort, as testified to by Fox (1975: 149): 'Language work overseas has shifted from a single-minded interest in teaching English to a realization that multilingual societies have acute language problems which are at the root of their cultural continuity and their political, social, and educational development'. Similarly, the French Government, which had long practised French only as a medium in its former colonies and had continued to support education through this medium, is now reported to favour a transitional type of bilingualism in which African languages are used as media of instruction for two or three years, giving way to French as a medium of instruction.[40] Although the motivation for this is the expectation that French will be better taught as a result, at least there is a recognition that plunging into the teaching of a second language hardly works, particularly when the classes involved are large and the teachers poorly trained. A recent admission of the failure of earlier policies is the concern expressed in French Government circles about the falling standard of French in black African and Indian Ocean countries and the plan to take remedial action, including new programmes and the target of one book for every pupil, five books for every teacher and one library for every school.[41]

Among African countries that currently use French as their only medium but have plans to introduce a mother tongue medium as well are Togo and Mali, which have begun to train teachers for this purpose and start experimentation in selected schools, and Senegal, which is proposing a model under which French will be introduced as a subject in the second year of Primary education, but used as a shared medium with Wolof in the third to the sixth year. In Sierra Leone, where the policy had been to use English as a medium for all classes, a pilot project covering twenty-six schools was launched in 1979 in the use of three languages, Mende, Temne and Limba, as media of instruction in the first three years of primary education.[42]

Innovations in mother tongue education can be seen as departures from the norm of playing down such education as a result of the survival of old policies. These innovations may be related to the status of a language: whether the languages are dominant, non-dominant or minority languages.

Dominant languages are the easiest to carry out innovations in, particularly in terms of their use as media of instruction. This is because such languages tend to have a good literary tradition as well as a sizeable school population to justify extensive provision of textbooks in the various subjects which the language is used for teaching. There is also a ready pool of potential teachers.

The pattern of the use of African languages as media of instruction in the former English colonies was usually the mother tongue or a language of the immediate community in the first three years of primary education, with English being taught as a subject and later becoming the medium of instruction from the fourth year. As we have seen, this pattern has survived unchanged in many of these countries; and, in some, a change has even occurred in the direction of elimination of the use of African languages as media of instruction. The major innovation that took place in the post-independence period was a move in the direction of extending the use of indigenous languages as media of instruction beyond the third year of primary schooling. For example, in Tanzania, where Swahili was already widely spoken, the language was used as a medium of instruction in lower primary education (Standards I-IV) and the first two years of upper primary (Standards V and VI). English was introduced as a subject in Standard V and became a medium of instruction in Standards VII and VIII. In 1958, the introduction of English as a subject was advanced to Standard III. In 1970, the introduction of English as a subject was further advanced to Standard I, but its use as a medium was replaced by Swahili for the entire primary education.[43]

Somalia provides another example of innovation in mother tongue education. Afflicted by two systems of education (English in the north and Italian in the south) as a result of colonialism, and three forms of competing scripts, the country was able to break away from the inherited practices and embark on the use of Somali as a medium of education. Today Somali is not only the medium of all primary education, it is also the medium of all secondary education, except for the last two years. From that point on to university level, English becomes the medium of instruction, except for the teaching of Somali language and literature.[44]

One innovation which has become famous in the literature on bilingual education is the Six Year Primary Project in Yoruba, one of the three major languages in Nigeria. Against the background of larger classes (caused by the introduction of universal free primary education), untrained and poorly trained teachers, inadequate materials, teacher shortage, poor supervision and outmoded curriculum, complaints began to be made about the quality of the products of primary education, who many felt were literate neither in Yoruba nor in English. The practice of making every primary teacher teach all subjects including English appeared to work fairly well when classes were small and supervision more effective. In the new situation of overcrowded classes, the resulting inadequacies were entirely predictable. Besides, since primary education was terminal for most children and the drop-out rate was as high as 40%,[45] the question arose whether it was not better to concentrate on the kind of training that would ensure the acquisition of some knowledge, at least in one language.

The immediate motivation of the Six Year Primary Project was a desire to improve the teaching of English. Following the report in 1966 of a Survey on English Language Teaching in Nigeria which recommended that experimentation should be embarked upon to determine the most effective approach to the introduction of English both as a subject and a medium of instruction in primary schools,[46] the Ford Foundation accepted a proposal by the Institute of Education, University of Ifẹ, Ile-Ifẹ to mount the project which started on the assumption that to improve English teaching, serious attention should be paid as well to the teaching of Yoruba.

The objective of the Six Year Primary Project was to compare the traditional system of mixed media with a new system in which Yoruba was used as a medium of instruction for the full six years of primary education. The experiment began in 1970 at a rural school in Ile-Ifẹ (St Stephen's School) with two experimental classes and one control group. The experimental classes were taught all subjects in Yoruba, except for English which was taught by a specialist teacher of English. The control group was taught in Yoruba for three years and later in English. In order to reduce the variables between the groups, the new curriculum and materials developed for the project were used for both groups. In 1973, the scheme was extended to ten other schools, this time including urban schools, and other variables were added, such as the new experimental classes no longer having specialist teachers of English and the new control classes no longer using new English materials. In addition, a third control group (the traditional control group) was added which used both the traditional curriculum and the old English materials. Table 3.2 shows the difference between the treatment groups.

All the groups were systematically evaluated from 1976 to 1978, and the results showed very clearly the superiority of the original experimental group in all areas - English, Yoruba, science, social and cultural studies, and mathematics - closely followed by the new experimental group. In all cases, the traditional control group was the worst. Although the influence of the new materials and curriculum is clearly in evidence in this project, over and above this is the superior performance of the experimental groups which could only have been due to the use of Yoruba as a medium of instruction.[47]

The lesson to be learnt from the Six Year Primary Project is that where a language is dominant, mother tongue education involving the use of an indigenous language as a medium of instruction for the entire primary education can be achieved without sacrificing proficiency in a LWC, in this case English, which is taught as a subject throughout primary education. In order to achieve this result, attitudes to both languages have to be positive. In Tanzania, it is reported that because of the nationalist attitudes to Swahili, the teaching of English has suffered in some respects. The goal of teaching English is said to be acquisition of 'permanent reading knowledge' by primary school leavers. This in turn means that less attention is paid to speaking skills. Since there is not much opportunity for children to use English both in and outside the primary school, the net outcome of the mother tongue education policy is likely to be a fall in the standard of English.[48]

While dominant languages such as Swahili, Somali and Yoruba can be used as media of instruction for the entire primary education, non-dominant languages can only be used as media for part of primary education. This is because they lack the population base and the status to support more widespread use. In Sierra Leone, where the innovation is to

Table 3.2. Six-year primary project treatment groups

Group	Medium	Curriculum	Eng. materials	Eng. teacher
Original experimental	Yor.	New	New	Specialist
Original control	Yor. + Eng.	New	New	Non-specialist
New experimental	Yor.	New	New	Non-specialist
New control	Yor. + Eng.	New	Old	Non-specialist
Traditional control	Yor. + Eng.	Old	Old	Non-specialist

Source: Adapted from Cziko and Ojerinde (1976)

introduce mother tongue education where none existed before, the plan is to use three languages, Mende, Temne and Limba, both for initial literacy and as media of instruction for the first three years of primary education.

A similar project in innovation in mother tongue education for non-dominant languages is the case of the Operational Research Project for Language Education in Cameroon (with the acronym PROPELCA derived from the title in French). As one of the countries in which primary education is carried out in a LWC (English in the West, and French in the East), the project is designed to experiment with the introduction of Cameroonian languages into primary education. Begun in 1981, the project sets out to try out initial literacy in the mother tongue and its partial use as a medium, gradually giving way to proficiency in the official language. Seven languages have been selected for the project and the following four, Ewondo, Duala, Fe'efe'e and Nso', are already being used. The allocation of functions between the mother tongue and the official language as media is as follows: reading, writing, and basic notions in arithmetic are taught in the mother tongue in the first year, the emphasis being on oral work, while written work in arithmetic, and more reading and writing, follow in the second year. Time allocation to the mother tongue gradually decreases from 70% in the first year to 30% in the third year. It is expected that at the end of the third year, pupils in the experimental classes would have a better knowledge of the official language than those in the control classes, while they would also be able to write in their mother tongue.[49]

It should be clear from the two examples of Sierra Leone and Cameroon that variations are to be expected in the scope of mother tongue education. While the Cameroonian model is designed to achieve a minimum use of the mother tongue as a medium, with emphasis on how such use will facilitate the acquisition of the official language, the Sierra Leonean model is more on the traditional lines of the intrinsic value of mother tongue education for its own sake. Such variations are to be expected in view of differences in the situations as well as governmental attitudes.

Minority languages, like non-dominant languages, lack a strong population base; but, unlike them, they exist in a situation in which there are one or more dominant languages. The tendency in such a situation is to play down their importance, particularly when the question of cost is invoked. Added to the question of cost is the fear of divisiveness associated with emphasis on several smaller languages. As has been explained earlier, divisiveness is a matter of attitude. It can be engineered, and language is only a useful peg on which to hang it. The question of cost is undoubtedly a serious one. In a situation in which the total allocation to education is inadequate, the priority is to concentrate on the major languages and LWCs. However, since the combination of all minority languages in a country may add up to a fairly high percentage, it would be unfair to ignore them in the educational system.[50] Besides, it makes good educational sense to exploit the child's first language background in initial literacy. To advocate this is not to 'fight a battle of rights', but merely to ensure that the minority child is given the best opportunity to make an orderly and meaningful transition from the home language to the school language.[51]

The Rivers Readers Project in Nigeria is one example of an innovation in mother tongue education involving the use of minority languages.[52] Begun in 1970, the project was designed to introduce initial literacy in about twenty languages/dialects spoken by small populations of primary school children and to use the languages/dialects as media of instruction for other subjects, except English, in the first two classes of primary education.[53] This experiment was also designed to replace the practice of using Igbo, a dominant language, which is also a lingua franca in parts of the area, as the medium of instruction. Although the absence of any objective evaluation and the existence of problems connected with teacher training and distribution of materials make it difficult to draw any conclusions about the relative merits of the new practice in comparison with the old one, two valuable lessons could be drawn from the project. First, costs could be considerably minimized by making use of uniform formats and illustrations for primers as well as cheaper methods of producing materials. For example, between 1970 and 1972, 40 publications in 15 languages/dialects had been produced, at a modest cost of 20,000 US dollars.[54] Such publications include primers, supplementary readers, teachers' notes, orthography booklets and dictionaries. Second, by harnessing community interest and participation, a lot more could be achieved. For instance, the Project enlisted the support of Language Committees comprising linguists and influential native speakers to review orthographic proposals and commissioned material, and to assist in the launching of books as well as general publicity for the project.

Obviously, the scope for the use of minority languages will depend on the situation in each case. While in some cases (such as the Rivers Readers Project) all the languages/dialects may be planned for, in others it may well be that only a selection will be made. Similarly, for some minority languages, mother tongue education may not go beyond use in initial literacy, while for others use as media of instruction in the first one or two years of primary education may prove feasible.

Innovations in mother tongue education may be characterized by three stages: Stage 1 (Proposed Innovations), Stage 2 (Experimental Innovations) and Stage 3 (Actual Innovations). The progress made in mother tongue education at primary school level in the post-independence period may be measured by the number of mother tongue educational practices at each stage as well as the role of the languages concerned. Table 3.3 illustrates the point.

Educational practices which have survived from the colonial period are not considered as innovations. Thus, the use of Arabic as a full primary medium in Sudan or the many languages used as initial or early primary medium in Ghana, Nigeria, Uganda, etc. are not considered relevant in this connection.

The fact that some progress has been made can be shown by the cases that have passed from the proposal stage to the actual implementation stage. This is particularly significant in the case of countries that never had any tradition of mother tongue education, for example, Guinea, Central African Republic and Madagascar moving from French as an initial primary medium to African languages.[55] The slowness of the progress is, however, underlined by the large number of countries that still keep to a LWC medium, the few countries (such as Zaire, Kenya and Zambia) that have moved in the opposite direction from a mother tongue medium to a LWC medium, and the innovations (such as the Six Year Primary Project) which have remained at the experimental stage for a long time, with little prospect of becoming a permanent practice.

Table 3.3. *Innovations in mother tongue education in primary schools*

	Full medium	Early medium	Initial medium
Stage 3: actual	Tanzania (Swahili) Somalia (Somali)	Mauritania (Arabic)	Guinea (Fulfulde, Manding, Susu Kisi, etc.) Central African Republic (Sango) Madagascar (Malagasy) Nigeria (Rivers Readers Project)
Stage 2: experimental:	Nigeria (Yoruba)	Sierra Leone (Mende, Temne, Limba)	Cameroon (4 languages cited earlier) Niger (Hausa, Zarma) Senegal (Wolof– Educational television only)
Stage 1: proposed	—	Mali (Bambara) Togo (Ewe, Kabiye)	Senegal (Wolof, Serer, Fulfulde, Dyola, Malinke, Soninke)

Mother Tongue in Other Education

The preceding discussion of mother tongue education has concentrated on the primary school level. This is because this is the level at which it is most likely that indigenous languages will be used as media of instruction. Beyond the primary level, it is only in isolated cases (such as Somali in Somalia) that this sort of practice is found. The role of African languages in secondary education is generally accepted to be as a subject. The scope of the teaching of the subject may vary from the lower classes of secondary school to a full-scale secondary course leading to a final examination as part of the School Certificate Examination. Such a full-scale course is found in quite a few former British colonies including Ghana (Twi, Fante, Ewe and Ga), Nigeria (Hausa, Yoruba, Igbo and Efik), Uganda (Luganda and Swahili), Kenya (Swahili), Tanzania (Swahili) and Zambia (Bemba, Nyanja).

The teaching of African languages in secondary schools is generally beset by problems connected with the curriculum, materials, time allocation, teacher preparation, and prestige.

The curriculum for the secondary school course in many African languages is based on an original pattern designed for foreign learners of such languages as evidenced in the old Cambridge Overseas School Certificate or the London General Certificate of Education examination with its emphasis on comprehension, composition, translation and use of proverbs. The prescribed syllabus is an examination syllabus and, unlike in English where an examination syllabus is further elaborated into a teaching syllabus, the teaching is mainly geared to mastering the content of the examination syllabus and sometimes even concentrating on points already tested in past question papers. It is not unknown for candidates to pass the examination by merely studying such papers or even in some cases for a non-native speaker to learn enough about the language to be able to pass the examination without much difficulty.[56] The result of all this is that the Ordinary Level (O level) paper in African languages is often seen as a soft option.[57] Although considerable changes are taking place, particularly as a result of the influence of the teaching of these languages in universities, with serious attention to grammar and phonology, some of the old features, including translation, still persist. It should be noted that a test of translation from an African language into English is more of a test of competence in English, while the reverse involves a test of competence in both languages.

The materials available for teaching African languages in secondary schools have largely been dominated by old-fashioned grammar-translation texts based on traditional grammar. Again, as a result of work in universities, the picture is now changing. Simple up-to-date grammatical descriptions are now available for some languages, but many of these are in English. There is a need to ensure that such texts are available in the language being taught. In literature, there is no dearth of literary texts. Some languages such as Swahili, Yoruba and Hausa have a surfeit of such texts. What is needed is a complementary set of critical studies of the works designed to make study of the texts potentially more insightful and interesting.

Time allocation is related to the importance attached to a subject in the curriculum. In many instances, African languages fare badly in terms of the time allocated on the timetable. Not only is the time allocation unfavourable, there is the added disadvantage that the periods allocated tend to be in the afternoon, when it is quite hot and the pupils are not very alert. The prime teaching periods in the morning usually go to English, Mathematics and other subjects considered to be more important.

One of the weakest points in the teaching of African languages is in the area of teacher preparation. In the past, it was believed that any native speaker of the language who happened to be a teacher in the school could teach his language. It was therefore not uncommon to add periods of first language teaching to make up the minimum periods of teaching required of any teacher. With the improvement in teacher training and the institution of courses in African languages in Colleges of Education, the situation has improved somewhat; but there are still cases of those who took only subsidiary courses in a language emerging as the specialist teachers of the subject in their schools or long-serving teachers without any formal training in a language getting appointed as group leaders of examiners marking School Certificate language papers. Educational authorities are now gradually realizing that teaching an African language is a specialist assignment in much the same way as the teaching of Physics or English. It requires adequate training in language structure and literature, in addition to a good knowledge of the language. In Ghana, a step has been taken which is worthy of emulation by other countries: a Specialist Training College has been established at Ajumoko specifically for the training of professional pre-university teachers of Ghanaian languages.[58]

Perhaps the most serious obstacle in the teaching of African languages in secondary schools is the low prestige attached to it. Teachers of such languages are not much sought after and, quite often, students do not consider them as proficient academically as teachers of other subjects. In fact, teachers of African languages often try to 'redeem' their image by making sure that they are able to teach some other subject as well. Since passing in an African language is not compulsory for most post-secondary studies and employment, it is usually only an optional subject which a student quite often does not offer. For admission to post-secondary institutions, and for all jobs, English is obviously a required subject. African languages are only required for courses in the language concerned or for jobs in which the use of the language is important (for example, in broadcasting). Even when a language other than English is prescribed in a qualifying examination or admission to certain institutions, the brighter students tend to go for some other language such as French (Latin used to be a popular choice, but it has now disappeared from the secondary school curriculum). As long as African languages are not required for specific purposes, such as appointment to the administrative cadre of the Civil Service or admission to the Arts programme of Colleges of Education, the question of low prestige will continue to affect the conditions and prospects of their teaching.

As an aspect of a bilingual policy, the teaching of a second African language is often proposed. Although in Ghana it was once suggested that a second Ghanaian language be introduced as a subject at primary school level,[59] such a scheme is clearly unworkable in view of the already burdensome language programme involving the mother tongue and English. Even a proposal to introduce a second African language at secondary school level, such as is to be found in Nigeria's National Policy on Education, is subject to difficulties connected with choice of the second language, availability of teachers, need for special materials geared to the teaching of the language as a second language, and time constraint in the secondary school curriculum.

In contrast to the situation in secondary schools, African language teaching is increasingly being taken more seriously in higher institutions, particularly in universities and Colleges of Education. Since the work of such institutions has also helped to improve mother tongue education at lower levels, these two aspects of the role of higher institutions will be discussed later in this chapter.

Adult literacy has always been a major domain for mother tongue education. This is principally because of the large numbers of the illiterate population and the virtual impossibility of providing literacy teaching in anything but the adult's first language.[60] According to the figures on which Table 2.2 is based, most of the countries in Africa fall into the range of 40–94% of illiteracy rates. In order to eradicate illiteracy in the shortest possible time, there is hardly any alternative to a mother tongue medium.

A few questions arise in connection with literacy programmes. Which kind of literacy? In which language (if not the first language)? How can literacy be made permanent? How can an adequate supply of instructors and materials be guaranteed?

Adult literacy was originally conceived as a process of learning to read, write and count. The emphasis was largely on the language skills, and the material to be read was anything of interest, but not necessarily related to the adult learner's work-life. This kind of literacy is now referred to as traditional literacy. Because of the serious problem of underdevelopment and the need to justify the expenditure on adult literacy, a new concept of literacy was evolved by Unesco in 1960, linking literacy learning to a learner's work situation and his environment. The assumption is that if a person sees the prospects of his economic interests being enhanced by literacy, he will be more inclined to pay serious attention to it. Thus, the cotton or cocoa farmer will be able to read about his crops, for instance when to plant, what fertilizers or pesticides to use and how to keep a record of his sales. The housewife will be able to learn about childcare, environmental sanitation and nutrition. From the point of view of the state, the spin-off will be improved health and increased productivity. This kind of literacy, which emphasizes the link between literacy training and development, is known as 'functional literacy', which has been defined as 'literacy . . . conceived as a component of economic and social development' (Unesco 1970: 9).

Although most adult literacy programmes now have a functional bias, it would be wrong to equate adult literacy with such concerns as agricultural extension, occupational training, health and rural development schemes. This is because the basis for literacy is still the acquisition of language skills and the widening of a person's horizon through reading. Certainly, there is a limit to how often one can enjoy reading and rereading literacy manuals narrowly geared to one's work. After some time, the newly literate person is bound to want to read something of more general interest. The point, therefore, is that while primary emphasis should still be on functional literacy, lifelong and continuing education demands that the newly liberated illiterate adult should be able to participate in the exciting world of knowledge which reading makes possible, and this can be done by the provision of interesting supplementary reading materials not narrowly geared to the learner's work or a given project.

Many literacy programmes have been mounted in Africa. These include the functional literacy programme in Mali, the adult literacy and mobilization programme in Ethiopia and Tanzania, and the adult literacy programme in Kano State in Nigeria, which won a Unesco prize in 1982. Practically every African country has an adult literacy programme. The Mali functional literacy project is one of the best known in Africa. Begun in 1967, the project took two years to plan and involved preparation of materials, harmonization of orthography, and organization into groups at different levels. Although it was envisaged that four languages (Bambara, Fulfulde, Songhai and Tamashek) would be taught, Bambara proved to be the strongest and most successful language, mainly because most people in the country spoke that language. The farmers involved were growers of cotton and groundnuts. As in the case of the Rivers Readers Project, community participation proved an important aspect of the programme. The organization was such that there was grass-roots involvement. Literacy centres were established, and, for each literacy centre, there was a literacy committee charged with the organization of the centre, including recruitment of organizers, enrolment of students, and provision of classrooms and materials.

The Mali project resulted in greater production, rural mobilization and development, and considerable interest in mother tongue education. A monthly newspaper in Bambara,

KIBARU, was also established, in 1972, for the provision of general reading. In spite of the success of this project, certain problems were highlighted: the narrow scope of materials geared to functional literacy, high drop-out rate, literacy in the mother tongue giving rise to yearning for unplanned-for literacy in the official language, and the problem of sustaining interest where farmers were involved in long-term agricultural projects.[61] No doubt, the way forward for African nations involved in literacy will be a judicious combination of functional literacy with a more humanistic and liberal application of literacy to a wider field of knowledge.

Although the medium of adult literacy is usually the adult learner's first language, situations could arise in which a departure from this practice could occur. A well-known example is the use of a widely-spoken community or a national language which the learner already speaks very well. This is the situation in Tanzania for large groups of illiterates who speak Swahili very well and are made to acquire literacy in it or in Zambia where speakers of Lenje and Tonga are made to use Tonga as a medium.[62] Another example is where a second language is imposed for adult literacy, even though the learners may not be very proficient in it. Again this situation may be exemplified by Tanzania in practice, where the policy is to use Swahili as a medium for adult literacy for all learners. Although there are obvious advantages in a practice that enables everyone to be integrated into literacy in a national language which, for that very reason, means access to participation in national life, a situation in which literacy is conducted in a second language puts learners at a disadvantage in relation to those for whom the language is a first language. The usual facilitation from sound to symbol will be lacking, and some negative effects such as inadequate literacy or semi-literacy and negative image of the mother tongue may even result.[63] In spite of additional financial costs, it is still preferable to begin the literacy process in the mother tongue, even if a transition to literacy in the national language is inevitable.

The problem of post-literacy activity is another serious aspect of literacy programmes. It is now an accepted fact that literacy cannot stop at the point of the literate's being able to read the simple texts that literacy materials contain. Supplementary reading materials are required, and these have to be interesting enough to continue to hold the interest and attention of the new literate. Without such materials, the skills gained may easily be lost and the learner may slide back into illiteracy once again. Permanent literacy therefore implies a continuing process of learning.

It sometimes happens, however, that literacy in one language leads to a demand for literacy in another. Examples are the Mali farmer who has learnt to read and write well in Bambara and who now sees his children who have gone to school reading and writing in French and so has aspirations to do the same, or a Tanzanian labourer who has successfully completed an adult literacy programme in Swahili and who now wishes to learn to read and write in English. This should be seen as an aspect of lifelong education, and although a state that is heavily involved in expenditure in the formal school system can ill afford to set up special schools for learners, special centres for adult education can be provided, particularly in urban centres for the equivalent of primary classes, leading to the award of special primary school leaving certificates. Such programmes already exist in some countries, such as Tanzania and Nigeria, under the auspices of Institutes or Departments of Adult Education.[64]

It is also worth noting that in addition to the Western tradition of literacy in a Latin-based script, quite a number of African children in countries in which there are large populations of adherents of Islam have their introduction to literacy through the Arabic script. This is particularly the case with children who do not have a chance of going to the formal schools. For those that do, literacy is acquired through a Latin-based script in school and the writing and reading of Arabic is then acquired in a Koranic school. This is the situation in certain parts of Northern and Western Nigeria where children go to such schools in the afternoons after the normal full day in the formal school system.

The last major problem of adult literacy is the question of provision of teachers and materials. With the high expenditure of many African governments on formal education, it is obvious that adult literacy can only succeed if there is a fair amount of community effort. The Mali functional literacy programme, for instance, depended on volunteer instructors and this has been the general practice in many African countries. But times are changing and the concept of paying an honorarium to instructors has become popular; but the honorarium paid is such that it does not really serve any useful purpose, since it is very low in value.[65] In the present economic climate of most African countries, the groups from which instructors could easily be drawn (e.g. primary school teachers) are busy supplementing their meagre income by farming, trading or some other part-time occupation. How can such people be attracted to take part in adult literacy classes, when taking part will mean economic hardship? Obviously, some more appreciable honorarium would have to be made available. The time is long past when adult literacy can be run solely on volunteer effort, and this includes not only provision of teachers but also of materials. If community effort is to be tapped, this could be linked to community development projects, for example through the government providing grants to match contributions in cash or in kind. Eradication of illiteracy is already accepted as a major goal in African political and economic development. This acceptance ought to be matched by a greater commitment in the form of increased funding of adult literacy programmes.

Developments in mother tongue education in several African countries have been due not to any deliberate policy decisions but rather to efforts made by post-secondary institutions, especially the universities. The major impetus in this connection has been research and teaching in African languages carried out by Departments of Linguistics and African Languages. Research has covered practically all levels of language including phonetics, phonology, orthography, syntax, lexis, semantics and pragmatics. Even in those countries that do not allow mother tongue education at the primary school level, research is geared to studying the languages for their own sake as well as as an aid to the study of the official language. For example, the Centre Linguistique Appliquée in Abidjan, Côte d'Ivoire has had a long tradition of the study of the main languages in the country, with a view to drawing attention to the problem areas in the study of French.

Research on African languages has led to the introduction of courses in language and literature in several universities, with the result that it is possible to take not only first degrees but higher degrees in such languages as Hausa, Yoruba and Igbo in Nigeria, and Swahili in Tanzania. Even in those countries in which such degrees are not offered, Departments of Linguistics, where they exist, cater for research in the languages leading to the award of higher degrees (Cameroon is an example of such a country where a higher degree in Linguistics is desirable for work on any language of the country). Where undergraduate programmes exist in African languages, there is usually collaboration with Departments of Education which provide courses in education, including the methodology of teaching the languages.

As a result of the programmes provided by universities, a core of well-trained teachers is made available for teaching in secondary schools and Colleges of Education. Thus, instead of just any teacher being assigned to teach an African language, the qualified teacher could not only get assigned, but also serve as a model to less qualified teachers in the same school. Those who teach in Colleges of Education also help to produce middle-level qualified teachers who are often assigned to lower classes of the secondary school. The net result of the initiative of higher institutions is that, in time, higher standards of mother tongue teaching may be expected. This is already happening in Nigeria. For instance, the first graduates of Yoruba were produced at the University of Ibadan in 1969. All of them went into teaching. Between that year and now, tremendous improvements have been felt in Yoruba teaching in schools as a result of the combined influence of graduates from all the universities. Through their initiative, a professional association has been established which provides a forum for orientation courses and also serves as a watch-dog for standards in teaching and examining.

Since the teaching of African languages and literatures is carried out in the medium of the language concerned, a challenge is posed for teachers to develop the appropriate metalanguage. This has been successfully accomplished in the teaching of Swahili in Tanzania by the Department of Swahili of the University of Dar es Salaam and by the professional associations of university teachers of Nigerian languages, with the assistance of the Nigeria Education Research Council, in the teaching of Hausa, Yoruba and Igbo in Nigerian universities. The metalanguage developed at this level is popularized by being used in Colleges of Education and secondary schools and the production of materials on the languages is facilitated. For instance, instead of different books making use of different terms, an agreed set of terms is employed in the description of language, literature and methodology.

Academic training in African languages and availability of a suitable metalanguage mean a widening of the base of possible textbook writers. For example, as a result of these developments and the introduction of a revised orthography in Yoruba, there has been an explosion of publications, particularly in literature. Graduates have learnt to collect, transcribe and describe oral literature. Some have gone into creative writing and a few have written course books on language.

One development of direct relevance to mother tongue education at the primary school level is the mounting of experiments by universities. All the innovations referred to earlier in this chapter – the use of Wolof in primary education in Senegal, the use of Mende, Temne and Limba as media of instruction in the first three years of primary education in Sierra Leone, the use of Cameroonian languages in initial literacy, the Rivers Readers Project and the Six Year Primary Project – owe their existence to the initiative of Departments of Linguistics and/or Education in the relevant universities. The paradox of mother tongue education in many African countries is that while it is negligible at primary level, it seems to flourish at university level. If any changes are to be expected, judging by current experience, they are likely to be induced from the top of the educational system rather than from below.

Other Tongue in Education

Although the emphasis of this chapter has been on mother tongue education, it is obvious that any language teaching programme must relate the teaching of one language to the others. In this connection, the other languages are the official LWC (for example, English in a country where the official language is English and French where it is French), a foreign LWC (other than the official language) and, in some countries, Arabic.

As has been shown above, the official LWC is usually a medium of instruction from upper primary to the tertiary level of education. This means that a great deal of effort is usually devoted to it. But there are problems associated with its role in education. Let us take the example of English. The increase in primary school populations has meant large classes and the difficulty of paying individual attention to children's work. The practice of each primary school teacher teaching all subjects has also led to poorer performance. An example of how bad the situation is in some countries is the report from Tanzania that 'most pupils in secondary school do not understand what they are taught in English nor can they express themselves in the language'. A secondary school teacher is credited with the following statement: 'We have 105 pupils in Form 1 this year. Out of these, only 12 can count up to 20 in English. Hardly any of them can form, or understand a sentence in English.' And this situation is said to be typical.[66]

Perhaps one innovation that can lead to some improvement is to make use of specialist teachers of English who will teach the subject in all classes. Where this could be coupled with late use of English as a medium of instruction, it is likely that children will only be exposed to tolerably good models of English, at least up to the point that they are then taught other subjects in English by non-specialist teachers of English. But perhaps more important than this is the problem of the creation of an adequate environment for the use of English. For most pupils, particularly in the rural areas, once the day's work at school is over, the use of English is also over. Even for urban children who have access to radio and television, it is receptive rather than productive skills that are exercised. If, as seems likely, opportunities cannot be created after school hours, it follows that the English class must have an in-built opportunity to use the language through various forms of play-acting. The drawback to an effective use of this strategy remains the overcrowded classes typical of a lot of schools.

One of the constant complaints in the teaching of English used to be inadequacy of course books and supplementary readers. Years of work in curriculum development and materials production have led to a great improvement in this area in many African countries. Instead of imported textbooks ill-adapted to the local situation, most textbooks are now written by local experts and they are fully adapted to the cultural and linguistic setting.

Another question that has become more important in recent years is the model of the second language that should be taught. English as a second language in African countries has developed its own characteristics. The teaching corps has been largely indigenized and, in most secondary schools, one cannot even find a native speaker of English. This means, in effect, that those who determine standards of correctness are second language speakers whose usage differs from that of native speakers. In the School Certificate Examinations taken by secondary school leavers, examiners often have to decide whether to accept or reject particular expressions. For instance, should they mark 'to wet the flowers', which most people say, as wrong and insist on 'to water the flowers', which is the correct native speaker's version? Increasingly, the answer is that due cognizance needs to be taken of variants which have developed in the second language situation.[67] Recognition of such variants is probably an easier matter in the case of lexical items and idiomatic expressions, but less so when dealing with contrasts in the English sound system. But even here, the time will come when institutionalized sound patterns will also have to be accepted as an aspect of English as a second language.

The teaching of English in higher institutions can be oriented towards an improvement of its teaching at lower levels. This has been the experience with the teaching of African languages. In universities, however, the inherited tradition of English teaching has been that of a first language situation where 'English' largely means 'English literature'. Although a few universities now emphasize English as a Second Language and provide specific courses in it for a Master of Arts degree, the old practice still survives in many others. When a graduate of English has spent practically all his time on literature, and goes out to teach in a secondary school, what he teaches in and about the English language is simply what he remembers his teachers to have taught at that level. Usually, he slavishly follows the teacher's book and displays hardly any initiative in presentation or explanation. It is important that English in the universities should be a combination of language and literature. If possible, the practice adopted in some universities by which students can have either a 'language emphasis' or a 'literature emphasis' in their first degree should be adopted. In any case, no graduate of English should follow a programme that does not include some courses in language, particularly the sound system and grammatical structure.

Because of the way official LWCs are distributed on the African continent, several countries often find themselves surrounded by neighbours that have a different official language. For example, Nigeria is bordered by Niger to the North, Benin Republic to the West and Chad and Cameroon to the East (all having French as an official language); Ghana has Burkina Faso to the North, Côte d'Ivoire to the West and Togo to the East (all having French as an official language). It is, therefore, natural that both Nigeria and Ghana should want

French to feature in their educational system. The usual practice is to provide for the teaching of French as a subject in secondary schools. A proposal was, however, made in Ghana for the introduction of French in the fourth year of primary education. Needless to say, this proposal never became a reality because of the enormous problems of implementation.

Even when limited to secondary school level, the teaching of French as a second LWC is beset by problems mainly connected with availability of teachers and the constraint of finding enough time in view of the demands of other subjects in the curriculum. In many cases, only a few secondary schools have teachers of French and so are able to offer the subject. Quite a number of such teachers are graduates of Colleges of Education who, though good in methodology, may not have been exposed to enough French to be able to speak it very well. The result is that many students of French in secondary schools acquire book French, being able to read and translate, but hardly able to speak. The question then arises whether the teaching of French as a foreign language should not be taken off the secondary school curriculum and limited to tertiary levels only. It is true, of course, that some African countries encourage English as a foreign LWC and teach it in their secondary schools. Senegal is one such country. Cameroon, of course, is in a special situation as French and English are joint official languages.

Where the teaching of French as a foreign language can be effectively carried out in secondary schools, there is no objection to the practice. Experience has, however, shown the inadequacy of French teaching in most secondary schools. The alternative is to shift all French teaching to universities and perhaps some polytechnics and Colleges of Education. That way, the number of teachers required will be limited; so will student numbers. A good job can be done by mounting intensive courses over a four- or five-year period. Although it is usual to prescribe a year of residence in a French-speaking country, such a country need not be France. Students of French in Tanzania go to Madagascar, while those from Nigeria, Sierra Leone and Ghana go to Togo. When numbers increase, even the cost of going to a neighbouring country may prove too high. A possible alternative which is being considered in Nigeria is the establishment of a language village where all transactions will be conducted in French. Students can spend their time in this enclave and, in addition to formal study, have an opportunity of using their French in practically all public domains.

Depending on its status in the country concerned, Arabic can be taught as a subject or used as a medium of instruction. In countries like Sudan and Mauritania where Arabic is an official language, Arabic is naturally a medium of instruction. In Northern Sudan, it takes on this role from primary to secondary education, and in Southern Sudan, from upper primary to junior secondary, while English takes over as a medium in senior secondary schools.[68] In Mauritania, Arabic is used as a medium of instruction along with French. The practice of using Arabic as a medium in a first language situation is not different from that form of mother tongue education in which an African language is used. There is a second possibility of the use of Arabic as a medium. This is in a situation where it is taught as a second language. It is reported that some private schools (médersas), mainly financed by friendly Arab countries, are springing up in some African countries (for example in Mali) where all instruction is given in Arabic.[69]

The most common situation in African countries south of the Sahara is the teaching of Arabic as a subject in those countries where there is a Muslim population, but where Arabic is not an official language. Unlike the teaching of French, there may be pressures for an early introduction of Arabic, even as early as the upper primary school level, because of its association with Islam. Whether this is practicable will depend on the availability of teachers. It would seem that introduction at secondary school level would be more practical. In any case, a distinction should be made between Arabic as an academic subject (like History or Geography) and Arabic as merely the memorization, reading and writing of the Koran which some Islamic teachers (malams) specialize in. It is the former which must be considered a proper subject of study in the formal school curriculum. And seen from this perspective, Arabic could even be offered as a subject by any student, irrespective of religious background or affiliation.

Language in education, as we have seen, involves different roles such as medium of instruction, subject, and initial literacy in the formal school system, adult literacy in the non-formal system, and the processes of socialization in the informal system. The informal system which concerns learning through parental or community guidance, interaction with sibling and age-group, etc. has not featured in the above discussion partly because the medium for it is non-contentious, being usually the mother tongue or home language, and mainly because its regulation is not a matter for the public domain. The formal and non-formal systems fall into this domain, and, therefore, questions arise as to which is the appropriate language at which level. This implies that each country has, or is expected to have, a language educational policy setting out the relationship between the teaching of the various languages and the levels at which they are taught. This is an aspect of language planning which forms the topic of the next chapter.

Notes to Chapter 3

1. Other possible questions concern how the language is introduced, and by whom and for how long it is to be taught. These will be subsumed under the discussion of the three major questions.
2. It is of course, possible to have Arabic as a mother tongue. This happens in African countries with Arab populations. In this role, the situation is the same as that of the first type of language.
3. This is an extension of Houis (1976: 397) to include adult literacy.
4. The problems involved in the Zambian situation are discussed by Ohannessian (1978a: 297–305).
5. See Mbunda and Brown (1980: 285).
6. This is a widespread practice in many situations of media transition. See Smock (1975) and Gorman (1974b: 491–6).
7. See Walusimbi (1972: 96).
8. For a previous account of some of these constraints as barriers, see Bamgboṣe (1985).
9. See Gellar (1973: 385).
10. See Rubagumya (1986: 284).
11. These arguments are advanced by Mackey (1984: 44, 48).
12. The notations L_1, L_2, L_3 not used in Siguán and Mackey (1987) have been substituted here.
13. See Bull (1964).
14. See Mackey (1984: 42–4).
15. See Bokamba and Tlou (1980).
16. See Raymaekers and Bacquelaine (1985: 455).
17. Some of these questions are discussed in Engle (1975).
18. See Unesco (1953: 47–8).
19. See Orata (1953).
20. See Dakin (1968: 27).
21. See Gorman (1974a: 435–7).
22. See Boadi (1976: 93).
23. See Lambert and Tucker (1972).
24. See Swain (1978).
25. See Bratt-Paulston (1974: 19) and Engle (1975: 19).

26. See Mackey (1978: 12-13).
27. See Bratt-Paulston (1974: 24).
28. The seven approved languages are Bemba, Kaonde, Lozi, Lunda, Luvale, Nyanja and Tonga. The problems posed for teaching by the policy of posting teachers is discussed in detail in Ohannessian (1978a: 306-12).
29. See Fox (1975: 118).
30. See Unesco (1977: 49-50).
31. The Togo case is reported in Weinstein (1980: 66).
32. Spolsky (1978: 59) draws attention to the difficulty of high technology being handled in languages other than LWCs.
33. See Hill (1980: 375).
34. See Mackey (1984: 45).
35. The test and its results are reported in Walusimbi (1972: 123-42).
36. The same outcome has been reported for the teaching of French. See Tadadjeu (1980: 71).
37. See Mulira (1951: 12-13).
38. See Szépe (1984: 69).
39. See Weinstein (1983: 138).
40. See Weinstein (1980: 72).
41. According to a recent article 'Language and invocation' in *West Africa*, 23 May 1988, p. 914, Jean-Paul Fuchs was commissioned by the French Prime Minister, Jacques Chirac, to report on the future of French in black African and Indian Ocean countries. He came up with these proposals among others to revamp the teaching of French in these countries.
42. See Johnson (1985).
43. See White (1980).
44. See Andrzejewski (1979: 6).
45. In fact, in a study conducted by the ILO in Western Nigeria in 1967, drop-out rates as high as 85% were recorded in some villages (Dunstan 1971: 571).
46. See Jacobs (1966).
47. For further information on the Six Year Primary Project, see Afọlayan (1976) and Bamgboṣe (1984a).
48. See Mbunda and Brown (1980: 295).
49. See Tadadjeu, Gfeller and Mba (1985).
50. For instance, Nigeria's minority languages account for roughly 36.8% of the total population, while Ghana's account for 44%. See Bamgbose (1984b: 21) and Ure (1981: 306).
51. This is a point emphasized by Pattanayak (1981: 75).
52. For further information on the Rivers Readers Project, see Williamson (1976a).
53. The school populations involved in this project range from the largest (42,000 pupils) in the case of Ikwere to the smallest (200 pupils) in the case of Degema. See Williamson (1979).
54. This compares favourably with an earlier estimate by Armstrong (1968: 234) which puts the cost of developing a single language at 15,000 US dollars a year for five years at 1964 prices.

55. Information on Francophone Africa is largely drawn from Weinstein (1980).
56. Walusimbi (1972: 97) makes this point in relation to Luganda in Uganda.
57. The feeling that African languages are a 'soft option' is widespread. See Boadi (1976: 107-8) and Ohannessian (1978b: 367).
58. See Boadi (1976: 106).
59. See Boadi (1976: 99).
60. In Section 3 of Mann and Dalby (1987), it is stated that most indigenous languages in Africa that have a standard orthography are used in adult literacy.
61. A full account of the Mali project is to be found in Dumont (1973).
62. See Kashoki (1978: 420).
63. For a critique of literacy in a second language, see Srivastava (1984: 35).
64. For information on Tanzania, see Hill (1980: 374).
65. The problem of poor honoraria for adult literacy instructors is a well-known one. See Bamgboṣe (1976: 25) and Kashoki (1978: 413).
66. These statements are from Rubagumya (1986: 290).
67. Even in situations where French is the official LWC and the practice has been to teach the metropolitan variety of the language, it is reported that attitudes are changing and local varieties are becoming popular. See Weinstein (1980: 70-1) concerning this development in Congo, where students resist correction of their local variety of French.
68. See International African Institute (1981: 73).
69. Information supplied by Louis Brenner of the School of Oriental and African Studies, University of London (personal communication, March 1988).

4

Language Planning

Types of Language Planning

The basis for language planning is the perception of language problems requiring a solution. Such problems may include choice of language for specific purposes in a multilingual situation, expansion of vocabulary to cope with the use of a language in new domains, or orthographic reform. Because of the need to work out strategies for solving language problems, language planning has been described as 'the organized pursuit of solutions to language problems.'[1]

The scope of activities covered by language planning is very wide, but basically, there are two types of activities: those related to *language status* and those related to *language corpus*[2] (i.e. the body of the language itself, e.g. its sounds, spelling, words, phrases, etc.).

Language status activities relate to decisions on the role of a language in a country at any level. They embrace:

1. Maintenance, expansion or restriction in the range of uses of a language for particular functions. For example, should a language be used as a national, official, regional or local language? Should a language be used as a medium of instruction in education or only as a subject? Should a language previously used as an official language or as a medium of instruction be replaced by another language? Matters connected with such questions are referred to as 'allocation of language functions'[3] or quite simply 'language allocation'.

2. Language standardization which involves the development of a given dialect or a group of dialects as a norm for the language in question.

3. Revival of a dead language (for example, the revival of Hebrew in Israel).

4. Introduction of an artificial language (for example, Esperanto in Europe).

Corpus activities relate to steps taken to ensure that the language itself is modified to conform with the demands made on it by its functions. Such activities include:

1. Vocabulary expansion, which also includes terminology creation and standardization of variants of existing terms.

2. Changes in aspects of language structure (for example, the introduction of a decimal numeral system).

3. Simplification of language registers (for example, rewriting the language of regulations to make them easier to understand or introduction of simplified language varieties for special purposes).

4. Orthography work which includes creation of orthographies for languages hitherto unwritten, harmonization of existing orthographies, orthographic reform (including change of script and spelling reform).

5. Prescribing rules on pronunciation (particularly of new words), correctness of style and usage.

6. Production of language material such as primers, dictionaries, grammars, supplementary readers, translations and special manuals.

In language planning, it is usual to make a distinction between 'policy' and 'implementation'. By their very nature, decisions on language status are policy decisions. This is because such decisions generally have political or socio-economic implications, thus requiring that the government or its agents be involved in the decision-making process. Most corpus activities, on the other hand, are not policy but implementational decisions. For example, once a policy decision has been taken to use a language as a medium of instruction, the measures required to work out the necessary terminology, compile and produce textbooks are largely those of implementation. It is the area that is usually left to experts to deal with. But not all corpus activities are implementational. For example, a decision to change the script used for a language to another script is a major decision which will require government sanction. It may arise from a recommendation by experts, but the final stamp of approval must be put on it by the appropriate authority. One way of knowing when a corpus decision is a policy or implementational one is to apply the test of ultimate approval. If such approval rests with a body other than the experts, it is a policy decision; if not, it is an implementational decision.

Notwithstanding the above, language policy is used in this

chapter to refer largely to any planning on language status. In this sense, a language policy may be defined as a programme of action on the role or status of a language in a given community. In a multilingual situation, a language policy decision necessarily involves the role or status of one language in relation to other languages. According to Noss (1971: 25), there are three types of language policy: official language policy, which relates to the languages recognized by the government and for what purposes; educational language policy, which relates to the languages recognized by education authorities for use as media of instruction and subjects of study at the various levels of public and private education; and general language policy which covers unofficial government recognition or tolerance of languages used in mass communication, business and contacts with foreigners.

To the three-way paradigm official, educational and general may be added the distinction between levels of decision-making. Language policy formulation involves decisions that are taken at different levels. There are higher level decisions taken by the government, and lower level decisions taken by subsidiary government agencies and private institutions. For example, a decision as to whether a language should be a national language or an official one or whether it should be used as a medium of instruction in the school system is properly a higher level decision. Lower level decisions, on the other hand, are consequential or subsidiary decisions taken by ministries, government officials or private institutions. For instance, once the government has decided that certain languages are to be used as media of instruction, it may be left to a Ministry of Education to work out details of the levels at which each language should take on this function. Similarly, if the general language policy does not forbid the use of a foreign language in business houses, it is left to a subsidiary of a foreign company operating in a country to decide whether to use the country's official language or the official language of its parent company abroad for keeping its records.

Language Policies

Language policies in African countries are characterized by one or more of the following problems: avoidance, vagueness, arbitrariness, fluctuation, and declaration without implementation.

Avoidance of policy formulation is an attractive technique because it frees the government from the unpleasant political consequences of any pronouncement which some sections of the community may find objectionable. Besides, there is sometimes the feeling that language matters are not urgent and can be solved at any time; therefore, there is no need to hurry to make any statements of policy. Several African governments appear to employ the avoidance technique, as can be illustrated from the fact that very few African countries have definitive statements of language policy. Absence of a statement does not, however, mean absence of a policy. What tends to happen is that such absence indicates the continuation of an inherited policy, such as the policy on an official language. The following statement made in respect of Sierra Leone is quite typical:

No officially documented statement or national language policy appears to exist, but convention and practice have formed themselves into an operative yet elusive language policy. In other words 'everyone is doing their thing', but life goes on and indeed there continues to be life after mother tongue education and literacy.[4]

Failure to enunciate a clear policy is sometimes seen as an advantage by linguists. For instance, the fact that no language is proscribed means that the linguist can carry out his research on any language and even experiment with the use of such language in education. Missionaries have benefited from this state of affairs as it has enabled them to devise orthographies for many languages, and to produce primers and translations of the bible. While avoidance of policy formulation gives scope for private initiative in language planning, it is ultimately a negative approach as it falls short of clear objectives. Suppose materials are available in a language and have even been tried out, the enterprise will remain at that level, unless there is approval to use them in the formal school system. This was the situation with linguists in Senegal and their work on Wolof. When the materials were ready and they approached the government, they were denied permission to try them out in the schools; instead, they were told to make do with the large number of children who could not get into the formal school system. The linguists, of course, felt that if they tried out their materials with ill-prepared learners outside the formal school system, any failure might be blamed on the language programme rather than the unfavourable conditions under which the materials were used. The impasse remains unresolved, except that lessons in Wolof are now broadcast by Educational Television. All things considered, therefore, a definite statement of policy is to be preferred to avoidance of such statement. Given a known policy, its weaknesses can be examined and suggestions made for modifications. For example, Zambia's language zoning policy has been the subject of repeated criticism since in many cases it exposes pupils to instruction in a language very different from their first language and teachers to teaching a language they are not competent in.

Vagueness of policy formulation may be related in part to the same causes that bring about avoidance of policy formulation. If the policy is couched in sufficiently general terms, it may go down well, since it will be a 'catch-all' formula that may be interpreted in a flexible manner. Apart from the policy being vague, implementation is not likely to be a burden to anyone, since it may not happen. An example of a vague policy is Kenya's decision to adopt Swahili as its national language. The immediate motivation was political. The ruling party, the Kenya African National Union, saw Swahili as a symbol of nationalism. It therefore proceeded to pass a resolution at a meeting of its Governing Council to confer this exalted status on the language. The vagueness of the decision can be judged by the implementation steps recommended. These included the requirement that all Kenyans were to speak Swahili at all times with fellow Kenyans (a practical impossibility since language choice depends on several factors, particularly topic, situation, and role relationship between the interlocutors), that government business was to be conducted in Swahili, that all civil servants were to be required to pass an examination in the language, and that Swahili would be given greater prominence than English in the schools.[5] Not only are details of how these prescriptions are to be achieved not given, the opposite of what is recommended has been going on, without any notice of the contradiction involved. Far from greater prominence having been given to Swahili in schools, English remains the medium of instruction from the first year of primary education. Although Swahili is spoken in parliament, the country's official language in which records are kept and administration conducted is still English.

Arbitrariness of policy formulation occurs when a policy decision is taken without previous enquiry as to its feasibility or reference to experts who are in a position to advise on the matter. The decision may be taken by a ruler in his absolute discretion, a government (particularly a military government through the promulgation of a decree) or a ruling party. For example, an all-powerful leader may decree that his own language shall be the national language or that his own dialect shall be the approved standard of a national language. The impression is sometimes given that all that is required for it to happen is for the government or the president to say so. Language matters do not, however, lend themselves so easily to such manipulations. It is not the same thing as the president decreeing that a road should be constructed to link the capital with his village. That can be effected immediately, once resources for it have been provided. Decreeing, for instance, that one of a country's major languages should become the nation's official or national language, without the necessary preparatory or implementation processes, is bound to end in failure. So also is the widespread, but mistaken, notion that a national language can be evolved by marrying elements of several different languages to form a composite language.

The arbitrariness of policy decisions may be measured by the interval between the time the idea is conceived and the decision itself. The shorter the interval, the more arbitrary the policy decision is likely to be.

It would be wrong to suggest that all arbitrary language policy decisions are bound to fail. This is because a situation may arise when such a decision may prove to be a solution to a long-standing problem. The case of Somali in Somalia is one such example. At independence on 1 July 1960, the country inherited three competing scripts (Latin, Arabic and several indigenous scripts) and two systems of education (English in the north and Italian in the south). This situation persisted and there did not appear to be any obvious solution. No government before the 1969 Revolution was able to take a decision on a common script. Then, on 21 October 1972, the Supreme Revolutionary Council took a series of decisions. With immediate effect, Somali was declared the sole national language and the medium of instruction in primary schools. The Latin script was adopted as the official script, and the new orthography was printed in leaflets and distributed by being dropped from helicopters. Civil servants and members of the armed forces were required to learn the new script within three months and be examined in it.[6] Although the Somali Language

Commission had, since 1969, on instructions from the Government, been involved in the preparation of textbooks and literacy materials in Somali, there is no evidence that its work influenced the decision, which was a purely revolutionary step to provide a radical solution to a long-standing problem. As it turned out, the decision was a success, for, later, Somali as a medium of instruction was even extended to all but the last two years of secondary education.

Fluctuation in language policy is due to such factors as changes in government or party policies, and new ideas or practices recommended by commissions of inquiry or adopted on the advice of foreign organizations. Perhaps nowhere is this more in evidence than in educational language policy. The case of Ghana provides a good illustration of such fluctuation in policy.[7] Like other former English colonies, Ghana before independence had a mother tongue education policy involving the use of an indigenous language for the first three years of primary education.

In 1951, under its Accelerated Development Plan, a change was made from the three-year mother tongue medium to early mother tongue medium (basically one year) with transition to an English medium as soon as possible (interpreted to mean the second year of primary education), with the mother tongue continuing to be taught only as a subject throughout primary education. In 1956, the Bernard Committee, set up to investigate the feasibility of using English throughout the primary school, recommended a return to the pre-1951 policy of a three-year mother tongue medium. This was mainly because the Committee found that, contrary to expected practice, 76% of the schools reviewed did not use English as a medium at any level. However, a member of the Committee, Mr J. N. T. Yankah, submitted a minority report advocating an English medium throughout the primary school. In 1957, the year that Ghana became independent, the Government accepted the minority report and put into effect an English medium policy for the entire primary education. In 1963, a committe of educators observed that there were not enough competent primary school teachers of English to carry out the English medium policy. It therefore advocated a return to some form of mother tongue medium. However, the Minister of Education rejected the suggestion and reaffirmed the 1957 policy.

In 1966, a military government took over in Ghana and the

ruling National Liberation Council set up an Education Review Committee in 1967. This Committee recommended a return to the three-year mother tongue medium. It also made a distinction between rural and urban areas, recommending that, for the latter, the change to an English medium could start earlier. The Government rejected the recommendation and decided that the mother tongue medium should be used only in the first year of primary education – a return to the 1951 policy.

In 1970, a new government came into power, this time a civilian government. The new Government went back to the 1967 recommendation which the previous Government had rejected, and not only accepted it, but went further to propose that the mother tongue medium could even last more than three years if possible. In addition, the Minister of Education announced in November 1970 that, with effect from the beginning of 1971, every pupil in Ghana would be required to learn a Ghanaian language in addition to his mother tongue; and the approved second languages were: Ga, Nzema, Akan and Ewe.

In 1972, a military government took over again, and in 1974, a committee on education reform recommended a three-year mother tongue medium, a practice that was already in existence. The Ministry of Education accepted the recommendation and went on to propose that each child should learn a second Ghanaian language (again, not new, since this was already proclaimed in 1970) and that French should be introduced into the primary school curriculum in the fourth year (the only new policy decision which, of course, proved not to be feasible).

A review of the policy statements in Ghana's educational language policy shows constant changes in respect of the mother tongue medium: 3-year medium → 1-year medium → zero medium → 1-year medium → 3-year plus medium → 3-year medium (See Table 4.1).

With each change come problems of reorientation for teachers, procurement of new materials or resuscitation of old ones and the inevitable lag between policy and practice.

Declaration of policy without implementation can take one of three forms. First, a policy may be declared which in the circumstances cannot be implemented, and policy-makers are aware of this. For example, when a country declares that pre-primary education shall be in the mother tongue and there are no pre-primary schools in the country, clearly the policy is only

Table 4.1. Fluctuation in mother tongue medium in
Ghana 1951–1974

Period	Medium			
	Zero	1-year	3-year	3-year+
Pre-1951			✗	
1951–1956		✗		
1957–1966	✗			
1967–1969		✗		
1970–1973				✗
1974			✗	

Source: Compiled from information from Smock (1975) Boadi (1976) Agyei (n.d.)

for propaganda purposes. Similarly, a proposal to teach French
in primary schools when there are not enough teachers of
French even in secondary schools can be said to fall into the
same category. Second, a policy may be declared, and escape
clauses may be built into the policy, thus effectively giving an
alibi for non-implementation. Third, a policy may be declared
but implementation procedures may be left unspecified with the
result that the policy remains only on paper. The last two forms
of declaration of policy without implementation can be
exemplified from Nigeria's official and educational language
policies.

Nigeria's official language policy is enshrined as follows in
Sections 51 and 91 of the 1979 Constitution:

> The business of the National Assembly shall be
> conducted in English and in Hausa, Ibo and Yoruba when
> adequate arrangements have been made therefor. (Section
> 51)

A House of Assembly

> may in addition to English conduct the business of the
> House in one or more languages spoken in the State as
> the House by resolution may approve. (Section 91)[8]

The first thing to note about the policy is the way in which
escape clauses are built into the formulation: 'when adequate

arrangements have been made therefor', 'may', 'as the House by resolution may approve'. Although one can argue that such clauses are necessary in a legal document (for example to prevent someone going to court to seek premature enforcement), the net result is to maintain the status quo as represented in the earlier policy, which is that the 'business of Parliament shall be conducted in English'.[9]

In addition to the escape clauses, the policy does not provide any mechanism for implementation. Which body will make the necessary arrangements for the introduction of the major languages in the National Assembly? When should each House of Assembly make its resolution on the languages to be used along with English? How should the decision be implemented? The absence of such implementation procedures has meant that the official language policy has remained unimplemented. The National Assembly commissioned a Legislative Terminology Project which was to compile technical terms in various fields such as Education, Agriculture, Law, Public Administration, Science and Technology, Culture, Communication, Transport, etc. with a view to providing suitable equivalents in the three major languages. This was to be followed by the training of secretaries, interpreters, translators and printers. Although a dictionary was compiled, the rest of the programme became defunct with the demise of the civilian regime. In the case of the State legislatures, hardly any steps were taken to determine the approved languages.

One way of ensuring implementation would have been to set up some mechanism for implementation such as a Language Commission and to provide it with resources and clear-cut guidelines on its responsibilities. As soon as the necessary preparatory steps have been concluded, the Commission should report back and a definite target date should be agreed for the beginning of the new policy, even if it has to be initially on an experimental basis. For example, the use of languages other than English could be tried out initially in some committees. Policy formulation without a clear statement of whose responsibility it is to enforce the policies and adequate provision of resources to back up such implementation amounts to carrying on with an existing policy.

The other aspect of Nigeria's language policy is the educational policy. As stated in the National Policy on Education,[10] the main aspects of this policy are:

1. Mother tongue medium from pre-primary school until some point in primary education.

2. Two Nigerian languages as core subjects in the Junior Secondary School and one in the Senior Secondary School.

3. One of the three major languages to be taught where the language selected should not be the child's mother tongue:

The Government considers it to be in the interest of national unity that each child should be encouraged to learn one of the three major languages other than his mother tongue. In this connection, the Government considers the three major languages to be Hausa, Ibo and Yoruba.

The policy contains an escape clause: *subject to the availability of teachers*. But since all language teaching is also subject to the availability of teachers, one wonders why this point has to be mentioned specially in connection with this aspect of the policy. The effect it has had is that most States have simply ignored the policy, since they can claim truthfully that teachers are not available. It is not enough for this kind of policy to draw attention to a requirement; it should provide for a mechanism for implementation which will include training of teachers and production of materials.

Other aspects of the policy illustrate the problem of lack of feasibility and vagueness. Mother tongue education is supposed to begin at pre-primary level, yet this is one level that is entirely left to private effort. Pre-primary schools are private schools outside government funding and control; hence, they cannot be forced to comply with the policy. Besides, parents who send their children to pre-primary schools are usually not interested in their learning a Nigerian language. Rather their interest is that their children should learn to speak English as quickly as possible. Hence, this aspect of the policy cannot be implemented. The policy about mother tongue medium is silent on smaller languages or even community languages now not being used as media of instruction. Again, a serious policy should include guidelines on these matters as well as provision for implementation mechanisms.

From the examples of policies so far provided in this chapter, it should be clear that language policies differ according to the situation of each country. While in Nigeria, there are official and educational language policies without adequate provision for implementation, in Tanzania language policies are backed by such provisions.[11] The declaration of Swahili as the national language was followed by the following measures: creation of the post of Promoter of Swahili in 1964 in the Ministry of Community Development and National Culture, with the task of co-ordinating Swahili development efforts being undertaken by various institutions and the establishment of Swahili groups in rural and urban areas; the establishment of an inter-Ministerial Swahili Committee to hasten the formation of technical terms in Swahili and to publish the *Government Directory* in the language; the setting up of the National Swahili Council in 1967 with the general function of co-ordination and promotion of Swahili development efforts and dissemination of publications in Swahili.[12] Thus, the official language policy consciously promotes measures to facilitate implementation.

The differences in the situation in each country and in the philosophy of the government in part explain the differences in policy. This is why a policy that works in one country may fail hopelessly in another. Because of the achievements of Somalia and Tanzania, it is sometimes thought that their policies of aggressive promotion of their national languages ought to be capable of being emulated in other African countries. This is a mistaken view because there are conditions precedent for the adoption of a revolutionary language policy such as is typified by Somali and Swahili. At least three conditions must be satisfied: the language in question must be widely spoken either as a first or second language; there must be the political will and mobilization of the populace to support such a policy; and there must be a strong or revolutionary government to give the necessary impetus and backing to the formulation and implementation of the policy. This explains why other African countries have not been able to perform the Somali or Tanzanian feat. Kenya, for instance, has, like Tanzania, declared Swahili as its national language, but it lacks the strong population base for Swahili and the other two conditions. Senegal has a strong population base for Wolof, but lacks the other two conditions. The Republic of Congo has a revolutionary government but lacks a strong population base for any of its languages and perhaps the political will. Thus, each country's policy must be based on what is feasible rather than what is ideal.

Perhaps the only area of comparability of language policies in Africa is the growing consensus on a *three-language model* to which reference has already been made in relation to models of communication. Each country would seem to require one or more local or regional languages, generally the mother tongue or the language of the immediate community; a national language for national communication; and a LWC for inter-national communication. In the case of Tanzania, for instance, this model is interpreted to mean the various mother tongues for traditional activities; Swahili for schools, some government and party activities, and inter-ethnic communication; and English for higher education, administration and international communication.[13] Translated into educational policy, it means education in three languages: a mother tongue (or the language of the immediate community), a second African language (usually the country's national language) and a LWC.[14] Obviously, variations in the three-language model are to be expected. For instance, where there is no national language, a dominant language will have to be substituted and taught as a subject; where there is a dominant language being promoted as a national language, speakers of that language may be required to learn one of the less dominant languages as a subject; where a country is virtually monolingual, only two languages need feature as media of instruction. A three-language model does not rule out the teaching of additional languages such as a language of religion or an additional LWC as subjects.

Inputs to Language Policy Formulation

When language policies are not arbitrary, there are a number of possible inputs that may influence their formulation. These include sociolinguistic surveys, descriptive studies, pilot projects, commissions, conferences, and resolutions by inter-national organizations.

Sociolinguistic surveys are designed to provide information on the language situation in each country. Such information will include a detailed account of the location and geographical spread of all the languages in the country, number of languages and speakers, which languages are major languages, the genetic relationship and state of development of the languages, and language use in different domains. This sort of information is useful in deciding on an official language policy and ideally, it should be part of the process of fact-finding before decisions are made on which language is to be used for official purposes. A similar type of information is no less important for an educational language policy. For example, if a government is planning to choose a language as a medium of instruction, it would need to know how many people speak the language, whether as a first or second language, and in which domains, what proportion of the school population speak the language in question as a lingua franca, whether the language is already being used in education and to what extent, and what the attitudes of native speakers and others are to the language.[15]

The most notable example of a sociolinguistic survey in Africa is the Survey of Language Use and Language Teaching in Eastern Africa. The Survey covered five countries: Ethiopia, Kenya, Tanzania, Uganda and Zambia; and one of its main aims was the gathering and dissemination of information on language use and language teaching in each of the countries. According to the Director of the Survey, Professor Clifford H. Prator:

> Each of these country studies would attempt to provide *as much as possible of the basic information judged to be relevant to the formulation of sound language policies and to the effective implementation of policy* through the educational system and the mass media of communication.[16]

As it turned out, the Survey succeeded in gathering a substantial amount of data on the language situation in each country, language use, language attitudes, and language in education. This material was presented in five volumes, each volume devoted to each of the countries and with the uniform title 'Language in . . .' (e.g. *Language in Uganda, Language in Kenya*, etc.). One unexpected outcome of the Survey was that it did not have any significant influence on policy formulation. The reason for this will become clear later in this chapter.

Descriptive studies may be at any level of language, including phonetics, phonology, orthography, syntax, lexis, semantics and pragmatics. Such studies may relate to a single language or a group of languages as well as dialects of the languages. Since they are usually carried out by linguists working in universities and research institutes, it is generally believed that descriptive studies belong in the realm of basic research, with little practical application to such concerns as language policy formulation. Experience with such studies in Africa has, however, shown that they have three possible functions in relation to policy decisions: affirmatory, anticipatory, and exploratory.

Anticipatory studies are those that serve to promote policy decisions. Where there is indecision about a particular course of action, such studies may tilt the balance in favour of one policy rather than another. For example, where there is doubt concerning whether to introduce an indigenous language as a second language to be taught as a subject in the school system, the availability of adequate descriptive studies which could serve as a basis for the production of materials may sway the decision in favour of introducing it.

Exploratory studies are those that serve to widen the options that are possible prior to policy decisions. Even where there yet exists no intention of deciding on any role for a given language or a group of languages, the fact that descriptive studies are available should make each language a possible candidate for selection when eventually consideration is given to deciding on a role. A good example is the use of languages in initial and adult literacy. The Summer Institute of Linguistics has been active in a number of African countries, describing and reducing several minority languages to writing. Although the main objective of this missionary organization is the translation of the bible into these languages, an inevitable by-product of its work is the availability of materials that can be used for literacy work. Countries that wish to embark on literacy in such languages have wider options than they would otherwise have had, if these studies were not available.

Pilot projects are a useful device for testing proposed policies through experimentation. In the preceding chapter, several of such projects in the use of African languages in education have already been described. Such experimentation is usually an aspect of research carried out by universities and other institutions. It is even possible for a private body to sponsor such projects. For example, the project on the use of Iṣẹkiri in initial literacy in the Bendel State of Nigeria was sponsored by the Iṣẹkiri Land Trust and run with the assistance of linguists at the University of Ibadan.

Pilot projects are potentially capable of engineering policy decisions. In this respect, they resemble descriptive studies with an anticipatory function. Once the effectiveness of a project is demonstrated, it is expected that it will be generalized, and findings from it made the basis of a new policy. But because pilot projects are usually not directly sponsored by the government, the question often arises as to how favourable findings from them can be translated into policy. The fact that those who design a project are convinced of its findings does not mean that the government will be; and, if it is, it does not follow that a policy decision will be made. For instance, the findings from the Six Year Primary Project support an abandonment of the traditional English medium in primary schools in favour of a Yoruba medium; but so far, policy-makers have not formulated a new policy on the basis of the findings.

Commissions of inquiry, particularly on education, usually involve the role of language. Unlike pilot projects, they have the advantage that they are sponsored either by the government or some agency that is able to influence the government. Most of the pre-colonial educational language policies have been influenced by the recommendations of such commissions. Some of the best-known commissions are the Phelps-Stokes Commission of 1919, which in its report of 1922 recommended a mother tongue medium in the lower primary, an African lingua franca in the middle primary and the language of the colonial nation in control in the upper primary school; the East Africa Commission, which in its report of 1925 recommended a mother tongue medium for primary education and English at a later stage; and the various memoranda on education by the Advisory Committee on Native Education in Tropical Africa, which broadly recommended a mother tongue medium policy.[17]

Post-independence commissions are country-specific. For example, reference has been made above to the various Commissions set up in Ghana. As these examples make clear, the fact that it is the government that sets up the commissions does not necessarily ensure that their recommendations will be accepted. In fact, of the commissions set up in Ghana between 1956 and 1974 all but one had their recommendations in respect of language rejected by the government.

The one advantage that commissions have is that they give an opportunity for experts to have an input into the decision-making process, irrespective of whether their opinion is accepted or not. Even when a government has decided on a policy contrary to expert advice, at least it cannot turn round and claim that it has not been made aware of alternative courses of action. It is true of course that experts sometimes have their own prejudices. In the matter of language, there are those that see themselves as promoters of a LWC, and some are even actively involved in the TEFL/TESL (Teaching of English as a Foreign/Second Language) industry. On the other hand, there are linguists professionally concerned with African languages whose sympathies are naturally for a mother tongue medium. But even when allowance has been made for such a subjective element, it is still better to have the benefit of the reasoning that has led to particular recommendations; and, all things considered, having such views to go on before making a decision is better than having none at all.

Conferences on language with a focus on language policy usually conclude with a set of recommendations. Of these conferences that are relevant to the African situation in terms of policy formulation, we can distinguish between those that are sponsored by Unesco and the others.

Unesco, as an international and intergovernmental organization, has been well placed to organize seminars and conferences whose reports are usually couched in easily-accessible non-technical language and disseminated widely among member countries. The following Unesco-sponsored conferences are relevant to language policy formulation: [18]

1. *Meeting of Specialists on the Use of Vernacular Languages in Education, Paris, 15 November–3 December 1951.*
Through the massive evidence collected and its authoritative pronouncements in favour of mother tongue education, the Meeting has been influential in lending support to policies favouring mother tongue education. A report was published in 1953.

2. *Meeting of Experts on the Contribution of African Languages to Cultural Activities and Literacy Programmes, Yaoundé, 1970.*
This meeting examined the current use of African Languages and their values as instruments of educational and sociocultural development and suggested measures to be taken to promote such values.

3. *Meeting of Experts on the Promotion of African Languages as Instruments of Culture and Lifelong Education in Eastern and Central Africa, Dar es Salaam, 1971.*
This meeting was concerned with the value of African languages in the region as vehicles of culture, science and technology.

4. *Intergovernmental Conference on Cultural Policies in Africa: Languages and Oral traditions, Accra, 1975.*
This meeting recommended the choice of one or more

national languages, a more intensive study of the languages and the increased use of these languages as media of instruction and in mass literacy.

5. *Conference of Ministers of Education of African Member States, Lagos, 1976.*

This meeting recommended the indigenization of African education through the introduction and use of African languages as media of instruction.

6. *Meeting of Experts on the Use of African Regional and Sub-Regional Languages as Media of Culture and Means of Communication on the Continent, Bamako, 1979.*

This meeting recommended the promotion of languages spoken across national boundaries as a means of inter-African communication and their use for administrative, political and economic purposes.

A sample of other conferences includes:

1. *The Commonwealth Conference on the Teaching of English as a Second Language, Makerere, Uganda, 1-3 January 1961.*

The conference recommended the early use of English as a medium, preferably from the beginning of primary education. This recommendation influenced policy decisions in Kenya, Ghana and Northern Nigeria.

2. *The Leverhulme Conference on Universities and the Language Problems of Tropical Africa, Ibadan, Nigeria, 29 December 1961-6 January 1962.*

The conference considered papers on the language situation in Africa and came up with a set of recommendations on language teaching and research. Of particular relevance here is the detailed statement on the factors to be considered in the choice of a national language and the consequences of choosing a foreign or indigenous language.[19] This statement may be regarded as a blueprint for policy formulation in respect of the choice of a national language.

3. *The Conference on the Teaching of Ghanaian Languages, Legon, Ghana, 5-8 May 1968.*

The conference considered papers on the study of Ghanaian languages and made a set of recommendations designed to enhance their status in the curriculum.[20] A few of these recommendations, especially those relating to teacher training and examining of Ghanaian languages, have been implemented.

4. *The National Language Symposium, Kaduna, Nigeria, 31 October–4 November 1977.*

This symposium carried out a comprehensive examination of the language component of Nigeria's National Policy on Education and recommended modifications as well as implementation strategies.[21]

Resolutions by international organizations are far more powerful than recommendations from conferences, principally because the nations concerned are parties to the decisions. In the African context, the best-known of such resolutions on language policy is the Language Plan of Action for Africa adopted by the Organization of African Unity (OAU) Heads of State and Government in July 1986. The document is in three parts: Part I sets out the objectives of the Plan of Action which is basically the encouragement and promotion of African languages, Part II spells out priorities in policy formulation and implementation, and Part III concludes with a suggested programme of action.[22]

The OAU Language Plan of Action for Africa is directed towards five specific goals. First, the use of certain viable African languages at national, regional and international levels as official languages in place of non-indigenous official languages currently being used, and the adoption of such languages as working languages by national, regional and continental institutions; second, the use of African languages as media of instruction as a way of making formal education available to a wider population; third, the speeding up of mass literacy which cannot be achieved without the use of indigenous languages; fourth, the acceleration of economic and social development through the full mobilization of the nation's human resources which will also require the use of indigenous languages; and fifth, the fostering of national, regional and continental linguistic unity through bilingualism. Unlike some national pronouncements on language policy, the Plan recognizes the need to make adequate provision for implementation mechanisms, and to this end, it proposed the setting up of national language boards to advise on and execute language policies, and proposed a major role for national universities in language development and promotion activities. Above all, the Plan recognizes the need for provision of adequate financial and material resources to make effective implementation possible.

To the extent that the Language Plan of Action for Africa

exhorts member states of the OAU to formulate policies along the agreed lines and make provision for implementation, it is certainly a great improvement on vague and ill-defined pronouncements; but to the extent that the Plan is apt to be seen as a political manifesto which need not be implemented by member states, it has not achieved the desired objective of changing attitudes of governments and policy-makers in favour of wider roles for indigenous languages.

Because the different inputs discussed above do not automatically influence policy decisions, the strongest claim that can be made for them is that they are *potential* inputs to policy decisions. All things being equal, a language policy that has been influenced by one or more of these inputs is likely to be better than one that has not. There are several reasons why language policies may not be influenced by these inputs. These reasons, which may be regarded as limitations to the influence of the inputs, include: constraints on findings in sociolinguistic research, lack of dissemination of research findings, absence of follow-up mechanism for the implementation of conference recommendations, inadequacy of policy-makers and official inertia, frequent changes of policy-makers, and lack of political will.

Sociolinguistic research may be so constrained as to rule out certain findings which may be relevant to policy-making. The source of such constraints may be the known attitude of a government to certain language issues or the attitude of the researchers themselves. An example of deference to government attitude is the case of the country survey in Tanzania as part of the Survey of Language Use and Language Teaching in Eastern Africa. It is reported that it was not possible to ask any questions which might be interpreted as questioning the status of Swahili in Tanzania or encouraging a systematic study of the other non-official languages. This meant that questions on attitudes had to be carefully worded to avoid eliciting unfavourable responses to the learning of Swahili.[23] The position of Amharic in Ethiopia was virtually the same. Before the revolution, it was the sole national language and any question of discussing its status with other languages did not arise.

Constraints on findings may be imposed by researchers themselves. This often happens when foreign experts are involved in matters which might be considered sensitive or controversial. In the Survey of Language Use and Language

Teaching in Eastern Africa, while policy-makers in the various countries looked up to researchers to recommend appropriate and viable policies, the researchers themselves, being mainly expatriates, felt it was unwise for them to go as far as recommending the adoption of specific language policies, since the issues involved were largely emotional or political.[24] If more local personnel or other African scholars who might not necessarily be indigenes had been involved in the work of the Survey, this type of reticence would perhaps have been avoided. The Director of the Survey envisaged the possibility of expressing opinions when he wrote:

> The authors should not hesitate, however, to raise questions of opinion which they themselves have no intention of trying to answer but which seem to have been overlooked. They should feel free in many cases to point out the possible relevance of facts to much discussed questions of opinion. They should even be allowed an occasional expression of their own opinions in matters they judge to fall within their area of technical competence, provided that they make every effort never to present opinion as fact and that they resolutely leave policy making to the people of the country.[25]

This injunction does not appear to have had much effect. One of the best-known African linguists in the region had this to say about the reluctance to make sensitive recommendations: 'While I personally subscribe to this view of avoiding direct involvement in other peoples' responsibilities, the scholar can still do a great deal to provide 'indirect' guidance as to what options there are in a given situation.'[26] Obviously, if he had been a member of the Survey team, he would have pressed for some of the recommendations to address these so-called sensitive issues.

In this matter of avoidance of direct involvement, there is the tradition of presentation of findings with clinical objectivity without pushing any particular solutions. This is inherent in scholarly training in most disciplines, and linguists, irrespective of nationality, are no exception. While one would continue to insist on objectivity as far as *facts* are concerned, nothing should prevent *comment* (much in the same way as journalists argue that 'facts are sacred, comment is free'). The fact is that if the linguist presents with detachment all the facts and the factors to be considered in making some decisions and refuses to go beyond this to evaluate possible options or even to recommend a particular option, he may be forced to look on while less knowledgeable people pontificate on the virtues of an option he knows to be unworkable or disastrous. Linguists in the developing countries have a duty to express an opinion on policy options they consider to be desirable. The alternative is for them to continue to carry out policy research that may be useful but not used by anyone.

Lack of dissemination of findings from sociolinguistic research quite often means that they cannot be of any use as input to policy formulation. In order to influence policy, such findings have to be available to policy-makers, and quite often, they cannot reach policy-makers because the studies are inaccessible or they are reported in a difficult format or technical language. Findings reported in theses, dissertations, journals or obscure occasional papers are often not easily available, and, when available, circulate only among scholars. Besides, there is an expected format for scholarly publications which books and papers conform to and that also goes with the technical language of the discipline which, almost invariably, makes little or no sense to the layman. Clearly, scholarly publications must retain their usual format; but in addition to such publications, there should be simplified digests presented in non-technical language and specifically designed for easy comprehension by policy-makers.

Another serious problem is the time-lag between the completion of research and the publication of the findings. For example, some of the East African Survey volumes were published almost ten years after the completion of the research.[27] Even at conferences from which practical recommendations usually emerge, such recommendations often end up being filed away.[28] The net result is that scholars write for, and talk to, one another, and little of what they write or say reaches those who have the power to take decisions.

Useful as conferences, seminars and workshops may be, particularly in terms of practical orientation, there is the drawback that they are meant for experts and specialists who participate in their personal capacity and have no mandate to speak for or commit policy-makers. This is particularly true for international conferences on language such as are organised by Unesco. Although recommendations from such conferences go to the various countries, there is usually no mechanism for follow-up action. The experts return to their institutions, and the policy-makers in the government who receive the recommendations without having the background to them often do not take any action. A way out will be for experts attending international conferences to have follow-up sessions with policy-makers, particularly in the Ministries of Education. In addition, certain types of workshops could be arranged at which experts and policy-makers meet at regular intervals to exchange ideas and deliberate on language policy research findings and recommendations and their implications. The objective should be to ensure that policy-makers understand such findings and recommendations, with a view to enabling the findings to form an input into policy formulation.

Many officials whose responsibility it is to take decisions on certain policy options are ill prepared for such a task. Sometimes, an official is trained in a discipline far removed from language, and he is then called upon to decide on language matters. One instance of this is the case of a certain Deputy Permanent Secretary in a Ministry of Education who had to recommend to his Minister whether or not the Government should accept the recommendations of an orthography review committee. Since this official knew that the author was a member of the committee, he seized the opportunity to lecture him on what he believed was the best solution to the problem of representation of tone. Instead of tone-marks, he would rather have a letter to represent each tonally distinct vowel. When the author told him that this meant that there would have to be twenty-one such letters for vowels alone in the language, he was embarrassed and immediately terminated the discussion. Needless to say, the committee's recommendations were never acted upon, since, presumably, the official never sent up any advice to the Minister. Even when an official has been trained in language, his constant involvement in administration may result in his not keeping up with developments in the discipline. The outcome may be that what he presents as expert knowledge is nothing more than sheer prejudice and outmoded views.

Whether knowledgeable or not, officials in policy-making positions are subject to what may be called *official inertia*. It is a consuming desire to keep things as they are, so that one does not have to cope with the consequences of change. This syndrome has been well expressed in relation to language educational policy as follows: 'At the very top of government, officials tend to be more interested in official language policy and keeping the lid on things than in actually improving education, especially if this involves upsetting a number of applecarts simultaneously.'[29] This is perhaps the reason why the positive findings from the Six Year Primary Project have not been converted into a definite policy decision on a mother tongue medium.

Lack of continuity in the personnel responsible for policy-making may limit the extent to which language policy may be influenced. Findings and recommendations may be discussed with one Minister who may be keen on pushing the case and getting a decision made. Suddenly, there is a change of government or a cabinet reshuffle and he or she is replaced. One has to start all over again with a new Minister whose priorities may not even include such 'mundane' matters as language. In some countries, even senior civil servants are not immune to frequent changes in postings, with the same attendant problems.

Resolutions by international organizations depend for their effectiveness on political action by each of the member states that are party to them. The OAU Language Plan of Action for Africa recognizes this fact when it states that 'the adoption and practical promotion of African languages as the official languages of the state is dependent primarily and as a matter of absolute imperative on the political will and determination of each sovereign state'. Hence, the fact that a Minister has subscribed to an international agreement does not necessarily mean that his country will implement that agreement. Thus, although in 1976 the OAU Heads of State and Government adopted a Cultural Charter for Africa, Article 6(2) of which states that member states should promote 'teaching in national languages in order to accelerate their economic, political, and cultural development' while Article 18 urges them 'to prepare and implement reforms necessary for the introduction of African languages in education', the Language Plan of Action adopted ten years later laments that 'the majority of Member States have not taken the necessary practical steps to accord their indigenous languages their rightful official role as provided for by the Cultural Charter for Africa'.[30] Hence, there is a collective OAU position which member states have felt free to ignore.

It is quite possible that African countries find it convenient to subscribe to politically desirable resolutions on language which they have no intention of implementing. On the other hand, it is also possible that, like political manifestos, some resolutions cannot really be implemented in the short term. For example, a resolution to replace current official languages or to use indigenous languages as working languages at national, regional and international levels will take a long time to implement, and may not be capable of being implemented at all by many countries. Even the OAU itself is not exempt from the manifesto syndrome. Although the 1963 Charter establishing it stipulates in Article XXIX that 'the working languages of the Organization and all its institutions shall be, if possible, African languages', the Organization's working languages have remained English and French. Yet the 1986 Language Plan of Action for Africa still calls for 'the adoption without undue delay by the Organization of African Unity and the regional associations, organizations or institutions affiliated to it of viable indigenous African languages as working languages'.[31]

Language Policy Implementation

After language policy formulation, the next step is policy implementation. The scope of language policy implementation is very wide, ranging from actual language work to production of materials and training of personnel. For example, where a language is to be employed for a new function, such as use as a language for debates in Parliament, certain implementation steps will have to be taken: the vocabulary will have to be expanded and new terms coined for a wide range of fields, bilingual dictionaries will have to be compiled and translators and interpreters trained; editors and media practitioners will also have to be trained to operate in the language.

The task of implementation is usually left to implementation agencies which may be official (such as government departments or special committees) or unofficial (such as university departments, language societies and professional associations). The implementation machinery may be centrally co-ordinated or dispersed among several independent bodies. Implementation may arise from definite directives or it may be based on local initiatives on the perception of felt needs.

It would appear that there is a correlation between the strength of a country's language policy and the nature of its implementation machinery. Where the country has a well-defined language policy to which it is entirely committed, as evidenced by a definite implementation mechanism, the implementation agencies are largely official, their activities are co-ordinated, and definite targets are provided towards which they should work. For example, in the implementation of the Somali policy in Somalia, there are agencies such as the Somali Language Commission charged with the responsibility for producing school books and literacy materials, the Ministry of Education and Youth Training and the Ministry of Higher Education and Culture which are active in developing technical and scientific terminology, the National Printing Agency which produces textbooks in large numbers, and the Academy of Culture which sponsors the writing and publication of literary works.[32] Similarly, the Swahili policy in Tanzania is implemented by the Institute of Kiswahili research which engages in basic research, vocabulary development and publications, the Kiswahili Panels of the Institute of Education which are responsible for curriculum planning, the National Swahili Council charged with co-ordination and overall development of Swahili, the inter-Ministerial Council which is responsible for developments in terminology so the language can be used in administration, and the Writers' Association UKUTA, which is also involved in the cultural and literary development of the language. Overall direction and co-ordination of these activities is the responsibility of the Promoter of Swahili.[33]

For many African nations where language policies are couched in the most general terms, implementation tends to be left largely to non-official agencies which either act on their own initiative to carry out what they believe to be in consonance with the policy or in response to an invitation to participate in projects sponsored by an official agency. In any case, implementation hardly ever arises from a directive to effect certain policies, nor is there usually any form of central co-ordination. For example, Nigeria's official language policy about use of certain languages in the National Assembly does not specify any implementation agency; but the National Language Centre through funding provided by the Assembly has been trying to work out legislative terminology by making use of experts in the universities. The initiative for this work arose from a proposal by the Centre itself based on its perception of the implications of the policy. On the other hand, the educational language policy refers to agencies such as university Departments of Linguistics, State Ministries of Education and the National Language Centre without a definite statement on what is required of them or concrete implementation steps in regard to the policy. The result is that whatever activity is going on is on the initiative of university researchers and curriculum developers, without any co-ordination.

As already explained at the beginning of this chapter, most corpus planning activities fall into the realm of language policy implementation. There are four areas in which work needs to be and is being done to give effect to policies favouring the use of African languages as official or educational languages. These are: orthography, language teaching materials, terminology, and translation.

There are three major concerns in the matter of orthography. The first is the need to devise new orthographies for languages that have not hitherto been reduced to writing. In doing this, orthography devisers are guided by the principles of accuracy, economy, consistency and similarity by which all and only the phonemic contrasts in a language are represented, with each phoneme uniquely represented by only one symbol or letter in all instances of its occurrence.[34] The roman alphabet is now usually adopted with such modifications as the use of special symbols, diacritics, digraphs, special values for ordinary roman letters (e.g. the value *kp* for *p*) and spelling rules (e.g. *n* after a vowel to indicate nasalization).[35] In devising a new orthography, some attention is also paid to existing orthographies with a view to the use of similar letters for similar contrastive sounds. The task of devising new orthographies is being constantly carried out in connection with adult literacy programmes, the use of lesser-known languages for initial literacy, and in research preparatory to Bible translations. In respect of such translations, the Summer Institute of Linguistics is particularly well known for its work in reducing to writing several minority languages.

The second major concern is the need for orthographic reform. This arises from the fact that the orthographies of several languages were designed by amateur missionary linguists and other enthusiasts who had no idea of the relevant principles on which a good orthography should be based. For example, a language with a seven-vowel system is often represented in writing by only five vowel letters, and, quite frequently, English or French spelling conventions are used for writing African languages. For example, English 'aw' or 'or' for a similar-sounding vowel or French 'ou' for a 'u' sound. Given this sort of situation, it becomes necessary to carry out orthographic reform in order to make writing and reading of the language easier.

Divergence in the way a language is written may also be the cause of orthographic reform. Such divergence can arise in several ways. Conflicting conventions may be used giving rise to uncertainty by writers and consequently differences in spelling of particular words or different conventions for word division and punctuation. Rivalry between Christian missions has been known to be the cause of divergent spellings. For instance, in Uganda, while the Church Missionary Society favoured the use of a diacritic to represent a long consonant, the Roman Catholic Mission opted for doubling of the consonant, with each Mission holding tenaciously to its own practice to the detriment of the language and the development of its literature.[36] Also in Cameroon, languages such as Bassa, Bulu and Duala have two orthographic systems: Catholic and Protestant.[37]

Another cause of divergence in spelling is the introduction of phonetic symbols to replace the roman alphabet modified with diacritics. Some of the earlier experts involved in orthographic work were phoneticians who believed in the superiority of phonetic characters and the difficulties posed by the use of diacritics. Hence they advocated the use of such characters. For example, the International African Institute's *Practical Orthography for African Languages* (1930), popularly known as the 'Africa Alphabet', introduced such phonetic characters as epsilon, gamma, inverted 'c', etc.,[38] which were used in the writing of such languages as Akan, Ewe, Efik and Igbo. The hostility to these strange-looking characters has led to spelling reform involving their abandonment in the case of some of these languages.

An orthographic reform differs from the devising of a new orthography in that the reformer usually does not have a free hand because of entrenched attitudes to the old orthography being reformed, and, consequently, opposition to the proposed reform. For an orthographic reform to succeed, the following conditions are necessary: the proposed reforms must be minimal, since the more widespread and radical the changes, the less the likelihood of their being accepted; as far as possible, each change must be valid for a wide area of the language; forms of spelling which have been long established must not be lightly interfered with; and the reform must have the backing of some authority, preferably governmental, which can engineer its acceptance. Examples of spelling reform in African languages include Igbo, Kanuri, Yoruba in Nigeria, Luganda in Uganda, and Shona in Zimbabwe.

Harmonization of orthographies is very much like spelling reform. It only differs from it in that a spelling reform may involve one or more languages, whereas harmonization necessarily involves more than one language. Harmonization of orthographies may be directed at the use of similar letters or symbols for similar significant sounds in different languages, or the use of identical letters for the same significant sounds where current conventions sanction divergent representation. Harmonization of orthographies may be carried out at the national level such that a stock of orthographic symbols may be prescribed for the languages of the country or a section of it. In Senegal, the stock of symbols for the six recognized languages is prescribed by decree. More usually, harmonization efforts are directed at languages spoken across national boundaries. For example, the Unesco-sponsored Bamako meeting of 1966 tackled the question of 'unification' of the alphabets of several languages including Hausa, Fulfulde, Mandingo and Kanuri.[39] Similar Unesco-sponsored efforts are the Seminar on the Normalization and Harmonization of the Alphabets of the Sub-Region of Togo, Ghana, Upper Volta, Nigeria, Benin (then Dahomey) held at Cotonou in August 1975, and the Meeting of Experts on the Transcription and Harmonization of African Languages held at Niamey (Niger) in July 1978.[40]

Harmonization of orthographies across national boundaries involves two major problems. First, the conventions to be modified are in use under two or more sovereign authorities and only persuasion and compromise can be invoked to make the countries involved give up existing practices. Second, those who are called upon to recommend harmonization innovations are generally experts in language or linguistics who do not usually have any say in decision-making processes at governmental levels. Hence, quite often, they propose or agree to certain changes which have no chance of being implemented. The point, therefore, is that international efforts at harmonization of orthographies without the backing of national authorities are of very little value.

Once an orthography is devised, it is usual to follow up such activity with production of teaching materials, particularly when it is intended that the language should be used in education. Primers, readers, supplementary readers and adult education manuals are usually the first types of reading materials to be produced, followed by dictionaries and more specialized texts, such as oral literature texts, history and legends.

Production of texts in African languages has long been bedevilled by the tyranny of the printing press. This is because most publishing houses in Africa south of the Sahara are more geared to printing books in English or French than in the indigenous languages. Printing texts in African languages thus becomes more expensive, since special symbols have to be designed and hand-set. A typewriter with a modified keyboard offers a way out of the difficulties of letter press, but even here, there is still the expense of producing copies by offset lithography. With recent advances in printing technology, it is now possible, by using a computer, to produce a wide variety of characters, even though the initial outlay is bound to be very high.

Wherever there is a project involving the use of a language in education, it follows that teaching materials are also being produced. These may range from simple literacy texts such as are used in the Rivers Readers' Project or a similar project in Cameroon to the more sophisticated materials of the Six Year Primary Project to which reference has been made in Chapter Three.

Work on terminology is a more advanced stage of corpus planning. Once it is known that a language is to be used for more than just initial literacy and as an official language, it becomes necessary to ensure that terminology hitherto expressed in a foreign official language is now indigenized through the use of certain strategies such as translation, composition, semantic extension, and borrowing with the consequent phonological and morphological integration.

Devising terminology for official purposes usually involves governmental initiative or sanction. Examples of such efforts are the Legislative Terminology Project in Nigeria which is concerned with finding terminology in the three major languages for English terms in various fields including Agriculture, Law, Public Administration, Science and Technology, Communication, Transport, Engineering, etc. This is to make possible the use of these languages as languages of debate in the National Assembly in addition to English. A similar effort in Tanzania is the compilation of the Swahili dictionary of law which sets out to translate English legal terminology into Swahili.[41]

For educational purposes, terminology may be devised for teaching other languages. Following an initiative in Nigeria, Unesco has been able to put together a set of mathematical and scientific terms used in primary education for which terminology is to be created in African languages. The strategies for such creation and possible guidelines on harmonization of terms across languages have also been agreed upon. In addition to terms for other subjects, terminology may also be devised for teaching language itself. Such terminology concerned with the language for teaching language is known as metalanguage.[42] Extensive lists of such terms based on the principles of transfer of concept, priority of internal resources, brevity and consistency have already been worked out for Yoruba,[43] and Unesco has further provided guidelines for creating metalanguage from lists of language terms for primary, secondary and tertiary levels of education.[44]

Translation of texts in English and other European languages was a well-known device for increasing the stock of available literature in African languages. The earlier translations were mainly scriptural - the Bible, the Book of Common Prayer, and related religious writings such as John Bunyan's *Pilgrim's Progress*. Most translations are still mainly literary, however, for example Julius Nyerere's translation of *Julius Caesar* into Swahili or Adeboye Babalọla's translation of Booker T. Washington's *Up from Slavery* into Yoruba. Although it is also important for technical and scientific texts to be translated as well, there cannot be serious efforts in this direction until African languages assume a wider role as media of instruction beyond the elementary level. Occasional efforts such as that of a Tanzanian economist who has written a textbook of economics in Swahili[45] are the exception rather than the rule.

Language Planning Models and Practices

Language planning practices in Africa have implications for language planning models. To what extent do they fit these models? Is there anything the models can gain from taking into account peculiarities in the African situation?

Haugen's original model consists of four stages: selection of a norm (i.e. selection of one of a number of competing languages, modification of an existing language variety or creation of a new standard); codification of form (i.e. establishing the selected norm by adopting an appropriate script, working out the orthography, describing the phonology, grammar and lexis); elaboration of function (i.e. expanding the language to cope with use in different domains, particularly developing adequate vocabulary for technological and scientific concepts); acceptance by the community (i.e. ensuring that a stamp of authority is put on the selected norm by users and the government).[46] Although it is correct, as some have done, to combine codification of form and elaboration of function into a single step (since both deal with language development),[47] this model continues to be useful as a general framework for language planning activities. The African situation fits into it well, although concerns such as allocation of language for specific functions which take up a great deal of language planning effort in Africa do not feature very much in the model as compared with problems of standardization and corpus planning.[48]

The actual processes of language planning dealing with such questions as who is responsible for selecting the norm and what the inputs are to the selection process are taken up in the planning model of language planning developed by Rubin, Jernudd and others. According to this model, language planning begins with initial fact-finding (which should cover all the information required for a rational decision to be taken), then there follows policy formulation involving establishment of goals, selection of means and prediction of outcomes, and after policy formulation comes implementation. At every stage in the planning process, evaluation takes place.

Language planning practices in Africa may be examined in the context of the processes stipulated in the planning model of language planning. The requirement that fact-finding should precede policy decisions is a reasonable one and, other things being equal, a decision arising from a full knowledge of all the facts involved is better than one that is based on partial knowledge or none at all. When dealing with corpus planning, no one will dare to suggest that decisions on orthography or certain vocabulary items should be taken without a thorough examination of known facts about the language and the implications of particular choices. In this respect, corpus planning activity in Africa is not very different from such planning elsewhere.

In matters of language allocation, however, the role of fact-finding before decision-making varies according to whether the decision is arbitrary or non-arbitrary and according to the traditional processes of decision-making in the country. Whereas, in developed countries, language policy decisions are expected to follow expert advice given by commissions of inquiry, such as the adoption of the Official Languages Act in Canada in 1969 which was preceded by the setting up in 1963 of the Royal Commission on Bilingualism and Biculturalism,[49] in African countries, decisions on language status are usually taken without such preliminaries. Again, in developed countries, some language status matters often have to go up to Parliament for discussion and approval, but in many African countries, one is not generally dealing with parliaments and democratic processes of decision-making, but rather with arbitrary decrees and proclamations.

What, then, is the role of fact-finding in relation to policy decisions in African countries? Fact-finding *does* take place, but quite often after policy decisions have been made. For example, the Survey of Language Use and Language Teaching was designed to provide information on the basis of which decisions could be taken on such matters as the following:

> Which language(s) shall be the official language(s) of government, used in laws, administration, police work and the armed forces? Which shall be taught as subjects and which used as the medium or media of instruction at the various levels of formal education? What language(s) must be accepted for use on the radio and television, in publishing, in telecommunications.[50]

But at the time of the Survey, decisions had already been taken by the countries concerned: Ethiopia had had Amharic as its official language for years; Kenya opted for Swahili as its national language in 1970 (although English continued to be the medium of instruction in schools); Tanzania declared Swahili as its national language after independence in 1961; Uganda continued with English as its official language and the main language of education; Zambia decided on English in 1965 as its language of education and its continued use as the country's official language. The kind of fact-finding which the Survey carried out is post-policy fact-finding. A lot of fact-finding work in Africa tends to be of this nature. A decision is taken and it is only at the point of implementation that experts are called upon to carry out the necessary fact-finding. The substitution of an English medium for a mother tongue medium in Zambia was a policy decision made abruptly in 1965. It was only after the decision had been taken that consideration was given to the necessary processes of implementation.[51] This, of course, means post-policy fact-finding.

Another type of fact-finding is the one that takes place after implementation has begun. This may be an aspect of an evaluation of how well the policy is progressing or gathering of information on whether the policy may even be considered to be feasible in the light of emerging outcomes. Studies on the effectiveness of certain media of instruction in schools and certain policies, such as the zoning of indigenous languages to be taught in schools in Zambia, are examples of this kind of fact-finding.

It seems, then, that, in the light of the African experience, the scope of fact-finding in the model of language planning ought to be extended to embrace three types of fact-finding: initial fact-finding before policy formulation, post-policy fact-finding and fact-finding during implementation as a result of which the original policy may be modified or even abandoned.

The planning model of language planning is based on the assumption that the processes applicable to social and economic planning must be applicable to language planning. Thus, the model provides for three things. First, 'goals are established, means are selected, and outcomes are predicted in a systematic manner'.[52] Second, the planning 'is characterized by the formulation and evaluation of alternatives for solving language problems to find the best (or optimal, most efficient) decision'[53] and third, in all cases, planning must be 'future-oriented; that is, the outcomes of policies and strategies must be specified in advance of the action taken'.[54]

Needless to say, a great many language planning activities in Africa, particularly language status planning, do not fit the rigid economic planning model. Decisions are taken without prior selection of means of attaining the objectives or a critical examination of the possible outcomes. In the model, the evaluation of alternatives is interpreted to mean not only that alternative courses of action are carefully considered, but also that a 'cost-benefit' analysis of alternative choices is worked out. This author does not know of any instance in Africa where this has been done before any policy formulation. Again, a forecast of outcomes even before a decision is made, as is generally the case in economic matters, is hardly ever observed in language matters, and there may even be some doubt about whether this is possible.

Language planners have been quick to point out that not all language development activities can be regarded as language planning. When conditions for planning are not met, we should be talking of a 'happening' rather than 'planning'. In fact, the term 'language treatment' has been coined to refer to all attempts to tackle language problems, no matter by whom and in what circumstances.[55] The question then boils down to this: does language planning take place in Africa or is what happens largely language treatment? Three possible answers may be given: language planning does not take place (except perhaps in certain aspects of corpus planning), since policy formulation does not conform to the requirements of the model; language planning does not yet take place, but it should and would when African nations have learnt to observe the requirements of the model; language planning does take place but the requirements of the planning model are too restrictive to recognize such planning.

The first answer is the one that most language planners will give. The second answer is the one some African scholars will give by way of apology for the failure of African countries to do 'what is right', as prescribed by the model. It is even sometimes suggested in extenuation that this failure to conform to the model is a temporary aberration which is likely to change, since, in any case, all African governments are aware of the value of economic planning as in development plans where the concepts of rational planning are in vogue.[56] It is difficult to agree that the current situation about language policy formulation is temporary. There is no evidence that decision-making organs will change in the direction of democratization such that arbitrary decisions will become a thing of the past. Also, although it is true that economic planning does take place in these countries, and presidents do not simply decree economic measures without consulting their advisers, the reason for this is that such measures have implications not only internally but externally as well. External constraints are such that a country cannot just do what it likes in the economic field without running foul of its international financiers, creditors and trade partners. Besides, the social and political consequences of arbitrary economic decisions are more likely to have an immediate impact in the country as compared with the effects of an arbitrary language decision which may take a long time to be felt because of tardiness in implementation.

The third answer is the one which this author favours. Language policy decisions taken without previous bureaucratic processes are no less an aspect of language planning. Their efficacy may be criticized, and attention may be drawn to weaknesses arising from failure to consider certain factors before decisions are made. But such policy decisions are a valid exercise in policy formulation. As Haugen (1983: 270) has pointed out, a policy decision 'may be preceded by lengthy wrangling in public or private, and it may be arrived at by some kind of majority decision. But it may also be decreed overnight, as when Ataturk changed Turkish spelling from Arabic to Roman'. It is even doubtful in general whether, in language planning, outcomes can even be accurately predicted. This is because language planning involves societal and idiosyncratic aspects of language behaviour. To that extent, the outcomes are unpredictable. As the social scientists Rittel and Webber (1973) have observed, there is an important difference between problems in natural sciences which are 'tame problems' and those in the social sciences which are 'wicked problems'. The latter admit of no definite formulation, there is no set of potential or correct solutions to them, and the problems are never really solved since each problem is a symptom of another one. Given that the nature of social planning is like this, it is doubtful if the rigid processes of the planning model of language planning can be sustained. What is more likely is that these processes may have to be relaxed to accommodate different kinds of policy decisions. The alternative will be to exclude much of language status planning.

The planning model of language planning assumes that language planning is carried out by a government or its agencies and usually at the instance of a central authority. The definition of language planning is said to be restricted 'to that kind of treatment which is governmental and close to the planning ideal'[57] and language decisions taken by non-governmental agencies such as private companies, media houses, language societies and individual authors are excluded from the realm of language planning.[58] Applying this constraint to language planning activities in Africa, perhaps well over three-quarters of language development activities will be ruled out, since they are carried out by non-governmental agencies often without express authorization or directive.

Although, by their very nature, certain policy decisions can only be taken by the government (for example, a decision to declare a language the country's national language), it is mistaken to limit language planning to government agencies only. Even with governmental planning, different levels of government may be involved (federal, state, local, etc.) and there may be conflicting interests and policy decisions. Besides, decisions taken at one level of government may have to be implemented at another level and this sometimes leads to distortion or failure in implementation.[59] For example, the language policies in Nigeria's National Policy on Education are promulgated by the Federal Government; but the implementation of practically all of them depends on State governments which control primary and secondary education. This explains why many of the policies have not been implemented.

In order to make the model of language planning more comprehensive, due recognition needs to be given to levels of decision-making as well as the role of non-governmental agencies. In terms of policy formulation, non-governmental activities can serve as an input into decision-making, or they may derive from a general policy already laid down. The question will arise concerning when a non-governmental initiative qualifies as a policy. The test would seem to be that it does whenever it is adopted by the government. As far as implementation is concerned, any activity by a non-governmental agency designed to effect an agreed policy is to be accepted as coming within the scope of language planning.

There is no doubt that the planning model of language planning is useful in clarifying some of the processes leading to policy formulation and implementation; but, by trying to attain the rigour of an economic planning model, it becomes too restrictive and excludes a lot of language development activities. By taking into consideration the peculiar problems of language status planning which many developing nations are preoccupied with, it is clear that the planning processes do not fit the model very well. On the other hand, there is considerable similarity in corpus planning all over the world and, to that extent, there is a need at least for a model that can account for this fact.

In attempting to solve the problem of the disparity in language planning activities and the wide range of language planning practices that do not fit the planning model of language planning, it would appear that there are two possible options: exclude practices that do not fit the model or modify the model to include a wider range of language planning practices.

Exclusion of language planning practices that do not fit the current model of language planning can be effected in one of two ways: to separate status planning from the scope of language planning and simply treat it as *language allocation* for which no prior pre-policy formulation may have been made; or to maintain that what is not planned is a happening, and consequently any practices that do not fit the model are at best only *language treatment*.

On the other hand, the model may be modified to make it more flexible and more inclusive. Some of the possible modifications designed to achieve this objective are: recognition of different modes of decision-making at the policy formulation stage (including decisions that are not preceded by prior fact-finding); provision for fact-finding after policy formulation and during implementation; provision for hierarchical policy formulation and implementation; recognition of governmental and non-governmental language planning activities; and integration of language allocation (status planning) and corpus planning in a unified mechanism that is valid for both.[60]

Language planning models are still at a pre-theory stage in that they merely provide a description of what planners have done.[61] It will be pointless to limit their coverage to only certain types of activities by language planners or planning practices observed only in certain countries. The more of such practices the models can account for, the more valid they will be. The modifications proposed will make it possible for the planning model of language planning to account for a wider range of language improvement efforts at both governmental and non-governmental levels, and in the developed as well as the developing countries.

Notes to Chapter 4

1. See Fishman (1974: 79).
2. The distinction between status and corpus planning in language was introduced by Kloss (1969: 81).
3. See Gorman (1973: 72–3).
4. See Sengova (1987: 528).
5. See Gorman (1973: 77).
6. For details of the Somali language policy, see Andrzejewski (1979).
7. Information on Ghana's language policy in education is taken from Smock (1975), Boadi (1976) and Agyei (n.d.).
8. See Federal Republic of Nigeria (1979).
9. This policy is embodied in clause 54 of the 1960 Constitution.
10. See Federal Republic of Nigeria (1981).
11. The implementation agencies mentioned in the National Policy on Education are not given specific assignments in relation to the policies.
12. See Abdulaziz (1971: 166–9).
13. See O'Barr (1976: 42).
14. A three-language model is the basis of the 'functional trilingualism' proposed for African education by Tadadjeu (1980: 3–4). See also Brann (1981).
15. See Ferguson (1975).
16. See Prator (1975: 147).
17. For a summary of the recommendations of these commissions, see Tiffen (1968) and Gorman (1974a).
18. For Unesco conferences, see Unesco (1953, 1981a).
19. The report of this conference is published in Spencer (1963).
20. For the report of this conference, see Birnie and Ansre (1969).
21. For the report of this conference, see Bamgboṣe (1977/1980).
22. For all references to the Language Plan of Action for Africa, see OAU (1986).
23. See Polomé (1975).
24. See Prator (1975: 155).
25. See Prator (1972).
26. See Abdulaziz (1975).
27. Although Ford Foundation support for the Survey lasted from 1965 to 1973, the actual survey field work was conducted in 1967–1971, but the last two volumes *Language in Zambia* and *Language in Tanzania* appeared in 1978 and 1980 respectively. See also Fox (1975: 117) on the delays in, and escalating costs of, the publications.
28. A senior government official in a Ministry of Education announced at a recent conference that, while he appreciated scholarly contributions by academics, he had no time at all to read anything more than two pages. Therefore, any material intended for his attention had better be compressed into two pages!
29. See Noss (1971: 31).
30. See OAU (1988).

31. See OAU (1988).
32. See Andrzejewski (1979).
33. See Abdulaziz (1971), Mhina (1976).
34. See Wolff (1954), Bamgboṣe (1965).
35. See Williamson (1976b: 13–14).
36. See Mulira (1951: 4–5).
37. See Bot Ba Njock (1981).
38. See International African Institute (1930).
39. See Unesco (1966).
40. See Unesco (1981b).
41. See O'Barr (1976: 47–8).
42. See Bamgboṣe (1987).
43. See Bamgboṣe (1984c) and Awobuluyi (1989).
44. See NERDC (1988).
45. See O'Barr (1976: 46).
46. See Haugen (1966b).
47. See Fishman, Das Gupta, Jernudd and Rubin (1971).
48. It should be noted that Haugen has revised his original model by spelling out details of each of the stages, and reordering elaboration of function in relation to acceptance by the community (now renamed implementation). For all the refinement, the simplicity of the original model still has a lot to recommend it. Some of the elements incorporated in the new model are borrowed from others, and, as such, are not necessarily compatible with the original model.
49. See McConnell (1977).
50. See Prator (1972: 9).
51. See Duggal (1981: 77).
52. See Rubin (1971: 218).
53. See Rubin and Jernudd (1971: xvi).
54. See Rubin and Jernudd (1971: xvi).
55. See Neustupný (1974).
56. See Chumbow (1987: 20–1).
57. See Rubin (1973: 7).
58. See Jernudd (1973: 18–19).
59. See Tollefson (1981).
60. For an earlier proposal to this effect, see Bamgboṣe (1989).
61. See Haugen (1983: 274).

References

Abdulaziz, M. H. (1971), 'Tanzania's national language policy and the rise of Swahili political culture', in W. H. Whiteley (ed.) (1971), pp. 160-178.

Abdulaziz, M. H. (1975), 'Methodology of sociolinguistic surveys - problems of interpretation and implementation', paper presented at Montreal, 19-21 May 1975 (mimeo).

ACP-EEC Council of Ministers - Brussels 1985. *The Third ACP-EEC Convention signed at Lomé on 8 December 1984 and related documents* (Luxembourg: Office for Official Publications of the European Communities).

Adams, Don (1977), 'Development education', *Comparative Education Review*, vol. 21, 2/3, June-October, pp. 276-310.

Adiseshiah, Malcolm S. (1976), 'Functionalities of literacy', in Leon Bataille (ed.) (1976), pp. 65-78.

Afọlayan, Adebisi (1976), 'The Six-Year Primary Project in Nigeria', in Bamgboṣe (ed.) (1976), pp. 113-34.

Agyei, Y. A. (n.d.), 'Research design on multilingualism in Ghana' (mimeo).

Alatis, James E. (ed.) (1978), *Georgetown University Round Table on Languages and Linguistics 1978* (Washington DC: Georgetown University Press).

Alexandre, Pierre (1968), 'Some linguistic problems of nation building in Africa', in Fishman, Ferguson and Das Gupta (eds.) (1968), pp. 119-27.

Alexandre, Pierre (1972), *An Introduction to Languages and Language in Africa*, translated from French by F. A. Leary (London: Heinemann).

Allardt, Erik (1973), 'Individual needs, social structures, and indicators of national development', in S. N. Eisenstadt and Stein Rokkan (eds.) (1973a), *Building States and Nations*, Vol. I (Beverley Hills: Sage Publications), pp. 259-73.

Andrzejewski, B. W. (1979), 'The development of Somali as a national medium of education and literature', *African Languages*, 5,2, pp. 1-9.

Ansre, Gilbert (1971), 'Language standardization in Sub-Saharan Africa', in Thomas A. Sebeok (ed.) (1971), pp. 680-98.

Ansre, Gilbert (1976), 'National development and language', paper given at the 12th West African Languages Congress (mimeo).

Armstrong, Robert G. (1968), 'Language problems and language practices in West Africa', in Fishman, Ferguson and Das Gupta (eds.) (1968), pp. 227–36.

Awobuluyi, Oladele (ed.) (1989), *Yoruba Metalanguage*, Vol. II (Lagos: Nigerian Educational and Development Research Council).

Bamgboṣe, Ayọ (1965), *Yoruba Orthography* (Ibadan: Ibadan University Press).

Bamgboṣe, Ayọ (ed.) (1976), *Mother Tongue Education: The West African experience* (London: Hodder and Stoughton; Paris: Unesco Press).

Bamgboṣe, Ayọ (1977), 'Language in national integration: Nigeria as a case study', paper presented at the Colloquium of the Second World Black and African Festival of Arts and Culture, Lagos, 15 January–12 February 1977.

Bamgboṣe, Ayọ (ed.) (1977/1980), *Language in Education in Nigeria* (Proceedings of the Kaduna Language Symposium), Vols. I and II (Lagos: National Language Centre).

Bamgboṣe, Ayọ (1979), 'Models of communication in multilingual states', *Journal of the Language Association of Eastern Africa*, 4,1, pp. 5–18.

Bamgboṣe, Ayọ (1984a), 'Mother-tongue medium and scholastic attainment in Nigeria', *Prospects* 14, 1, pp. 87–93.

Bamgboṣe, Ayọ (1984b), 'Minority languages and literacy', in Coulmas (ed.) (1984), pp. 21–7.

Bamgboṣe, Ayọ (ed.) (1984c), *Yoruba Metalanguage* Vol. I (Lagos: Nigeria Educational Research Council).

Bamgboṣe, Ayọ (1985), 'Barriers to effective education in West African languages', in Williamson (ed.) 1985, pp. 22–38.

Bamgboṣe, Ayọ (1987), *A Guide to Terminology in African Language Education* (Dakar: Unesco Regional Office for Education in Africa).

Bamgboṣe, Ayọ (1989), 'Issues for a model of language planning', *Language Problems and Language Planning*, 13, 1, pp. 24–34.

Banjo, Ayọ (1975), 'Language policy in Nigeria', in Smock and Bentsi-Enchill (eds.) (1975), pp. 206–19.

Banks, Arthur and Robert B. Textor (1965), *A Cross-Polity Survey* (Cambridge, Mass.: MIT Press).

Bataille, Léon (ed.) (1976), *A Turning Point for Literacy* (Oxford: Pergamon Press).

Bell, Wendel and Walter E. Freeman (eds.) (1974), *Ethnicity and Nation-Building* (Beverley Hills: Sage Publications).

Berry, Jack (1971), 'The Madina Project, Ghana', in W. H. Whiteley (ed.) (1971), pp. 318–33.

Birnie, John H. and Ansre, Gilbert (eds.) (1969), *Proceedings of the Conference on the Study of Ghanaian Languages* (Legon, Ghana: Ghana Publishing Corporation for the Institute of African Studies, University of Ghana, Legon).

Boadi, Lawrence (1976), 'Mother tongue education in Ghana', in Bamgboṣe (ed.) (1976), pp. 83-112.

Bokamba, Eyamba and Josiah Tlou (1980), 'The consequences of language policies of African States vis-à-vis education', in K. Mateene (ed.) (1980), *Reconsideration of African Linguistic Policies* (Kampala: O.A.U. Bureau of Languages), pp. 45-64.

Bot Ba Njock, Marcel (1981), 'The transcription and harmonization of the transcription of African languages', in Unesco (1981b), pp. 64-94.

Brann, C. M. B. (1975), 'Standardisation des langues et éducation au Nigeria', *African Languages*, 1, pp. 204-24.

Brann, C. M. B. (1981), *Trilingualism in Language Planning for Education in Sub-Saharan Africa* (Paris: Unesco).

Bratt-Paulston, Christina (1974), *Implications of Language Learning Theory for Language Planning Concerns in Bilingual Education* (Arlington, Va.: Center for Applied Linguistics).

Bull, W. (1964), 'The use of vernacular languages in fundamental education', in Hymes (ed.) (1964), pp. 527-33.

Calvet, M. and F. Wioland (1967), 'L'Expansion du Wolof au Sénégal', *Bulletin IFAN*, XXIV (B), 3/4, pp. 604-18.

Campos, S. N. (1980), *Adult Literacy in National Development: A case study of a developing country* (Swansea: Centre for Development Studies, University of Swansea).

Capo, Hounkpati (1988), *Renaissance du Gbe* (Hamburg: Helmut Buske Verlag).

Chumbow, Beban S. (1987), 'Towards a language planning model for Africa', *Journal of West African Languages*, XVII, 1, pp. 15-22.

Colson, Elizabeth (1968), 'Contemporary tribes and the development of nationalism', in Helm (ed.) (1968), pp. 201-6.

Connor, W. (1972), 'Nation building or nation destroying?', *World Politics*, 24, pp. 319-50.

Coulmas, Florian (ed.) (1984), *Linguistic Minorities and Literacy* (Berlin: Mouton Publishers).

Cziko, Gary and A. Ojẹrinde (1976), *Yoruba Six-Year Project: The 1976 evaluation* (Ife: University of Ife) (mimeo).

Dakin, Julian (1968), 'Language and education in India', in Dakin, Tiffen and Widdowson (eds.) (1968), pp. 1-61.

Dakin, Julian, Brian Tiffen and H. G. Widdowson (eds.) (1968), *Language in Education* (London: OUP).

Das Gupta, Jyotirindra (1968), 'Language diversity and national development', in Fishman, Ferguson and Das Gupta (eds.) (1968), pp. 17-26.

Deutsch, Karl W. (1953), *Nationalism and Social Communication* (New York: MIT Press and John Wiley).

Deutsch, Karl W. (1963), 'Some problems in the study of nation-building', in Karl W. Deutsch and William J. Folz (eds.) (1963), *Nation-Building* (New York: Atherton Press), pp. 1-16.

Dore, Ronald (1976), *The Diploma Disease: Education, qualification and development* (Berkeley and Los Angeles: University of California Press).

Dua, Hans R. (1985), *Language Planning in India* (New Delhi: Harnan Publications).

Duggal, N. K. (ed.) (1981), *Toward a Language Policy for Namibia* (Lusaka: United Nations Institute for Namibia).

Dumont, B. (1973), *Functional Literacy in Mali: Training for development* (Paris: Unesco).

Dunstan, Elizabeth (1971), 'Language teaching', in T. A. Sebeok (ed.) (1971), pp. 570-86.

The Economist (1987), *The World in Figures* (London: Hodder & Stoughton).

Eisenstadt, S. N. and Stein Rokkan (eds.) (1973a), *Building States and Nations*, Vol. I (Beverley Hills: Sage Publications).

Eisenstadt, S. N. and Stein Rokkan (eds.) (1973b), *Building States and Nations* Vol. II (Beverley Hills: Sage Publications).

Engle, Patricia Lee (1975), *The Use of Vernacular Languages in Education for Minority Language Groups* (Arlington, Va.: Center for Applied Linguistics).

Federal Republic of Nigeria (1974), *Public Service Review Commission: Main report* (Lagos: Federal Ministry of Information).

Federal Republic of Nigeria (1979), *The Constitution of the Federal Republic of Nigeria 1979* (Lagos: Federal Ministry of Information).

Federal Republic of Nigeria (1981), *National Policy on Education* (revised) (Lagos: Federal Government Press).

Federation of Nigeria (1961-2), *Parliamentary Debates*, First Parliament, Second Session 1961-62. House of Representatives (Lagos: Federal Government Printer), columns 3145-78.

Ferguson, Charles (1962), 'The language factor in national development', in Rice (1962), pp. 8-14.

Ferguson, Charles (1975), 'On sociolinguistically-oriented language surveys', in Ohannessian, Ferguson and Polomé (eds.) (1975), pp. 1-5.

Fishman, Joshua (1968a), 'Nationality-nationalism and nation-nationism', in Fishman, Ferguson, Das Gupta (eds.) (1968), pp. 39-51.

Fishman, Joshua (1968b), 'Some contrasts between linguistically homogeneous and linguistically heterogeneous polities', in Fishman, Ferguson and Das Gupta (eds.) (1968), pp. 53-68.

Fishman, Joshua (1971), 'National languages and Languages of Wider Communication in the developing nations', in W. H. Whiteley (ed.) (1971), pp. 27-56.

Fishman, Joshua (ed.) (1974), *Advances in Language Planning* (The Hague: Mouton).

Fishman, Joshua (1978), 'Positive bilingualism: some overlooked rationales and forefathers', in James E. Alatis (ed.) (1978), pp. 42-52.

Fishman, Joshua, Charles Ferguson and Jyotirindra Das Gupta (eds.) (1968), *Language Problems of Developing Nations* (New York: John Wiley).

Fishman, Joshua, J. Das Gupta, B. Jernudd and Joan Rubin (1971), 'Research outline for comparative studies of language planning', in Rubin and Jernudd (eds.) (1971), pp. 293-305.

Fonlon, Bernard (1975), 'The language problem in Cameroon: an historical perspective', in Smock and Bentsi-Enchill (eds.) (1975), pp. 189-205.

Fox, Melvin J. (1975), *Language and Development: A retrospective survey of Ford Foundation Language Projects 1952-1974*, Vol. 1 (New York: Ford Foundation).

Freeman, Walter E. (1974), 'Functions of ethnic conflict and their contributions to national growth', in Bell and Freeman (eds.) (1974), pp. 177-86.

Gellar, Sheldon (1973), 'State-building and nation-building in West Africa', in S. N. Einsenstadt and Stein Rokkan (eds.) (1973b), pp. 384-426.

Giles, Howard and Bernard Saint-Jacques (eds.) (1979), *Language and Ethnic Relations* (Oxford: Pergamon Press).

Gorman, T. P. (1974a), 'The development of language policy in Kenya with particular reference to the educational system', in Whiteley (ed.) (1974), pp. 397-453.

Gorman, T. P. (1974b), 'The teaching of languages at secondary level: some significant problems', in Whiteley (ed.) (1974), pp. 481-537.

Gorman, T. P. (1973), 'Language allocation and language planning in a developing nation', in Rubin and Shuy (eds.) (1973), pp. 72-82.

Grimes, J. E. (1974), *Word Lists and Languages* (Ithaca, NY: Department of Modern Languages and Linguistics, Cornell University).

Haarman, Harald (1986), *Language in Ethnicity* (Berlin: Mouton Publishers).

Haugen, Einar (1966a), 'Semi-communication: the language gap in Scandinavia', in E. Haugen (1971), *The Ecology of Language* (Stanford: Stanford University Press), pp. 215-36.

Haugen, Einar (1966b), 'Dialect, language, nation', in E. Haugen (1971), *The Ecology of Language* (Stanford: Stanford University Press), pp. 237-54.

Haugen, Einar (1983), 'The implementation of corpus planning', in J. Cobarrubias and Joshua A. Fishman (eds.) *Progress in Language Planning* (Berlin: Mouton Publishers).

Heine, Bernd (1979), 'Vertical and horizontal communication', *Journal of the Language Association of Eastern Nigeria*, 4,1, pp. 106-19.

Helm, June (ed.) (1968), *Essays on the Problem of Tribe* (Seattle: University of Washington Press).

Herbert, R. K. (ed.) (1975), *Patterns in Language, Culture and Society: Sub-Saharan Africa* (Columbus, Ohio: Department of Linguistics, Ohio State University).

Hill, C. P. (1980), 'Some developments in language and education in Tanzania since 1969', in Polomé and Hill (eds.) (1980), pp. 362-404.

Houis, Maurice (1976), 'The problem of the choice of languages in Africa', *Prospects*, 6, 3, pp. 393-405.

Hymes, Dell (1968), 'Linguistic problems in defining the concept "tribe"', in Helm (ed.) (1968), pp. 23-48.

Hymes, Dell (ed.) (1964), *Language and Culture in Society* (New York: Harper and Row).

International African Institute (1930), *Practical Orthography for African Languages* (London: International African Institute). [Reprint KPI 1990]

International African Institute (1981), *Provisional Survey of Major Languages and Language Use in Independent States of Sub-Saharan Africa* (Paris: Unesco).

Isayev, M. I. (1977), *National Languages in the USSR: Problems and solutions* (Moscow: Progress Publications).

Jacobs, Robert (ed.) (1966), *English Language Teaching in Nigeria* (Lagos: The Ford Foundation).

Jernudd, Björn (1973), 'Language planning as a type of language treatment', in Rubin and Shuy (eds.) (1973), pp. 11-23.

Johnson, Alex C. (1985), 'National language policy and the Sierra Leonean languages in education', in Kay Williamson (ed.) (1985), pp. 55-79.

Kashoki, Mubanga E. (1978), 'The Zambia adult literacy programme', in S. Ohannessian and M. E. Kashoki (eds.) (1978), pp. 398-423.

Kashoki, Mubanga E. (1982), 'Language policies and practices in independent Black Africa: trends and prospects', in Afọlabi Ọlabimtan (ed.) (1982), pp. 9-27.

Kelman, Herbert C. (1971), 'Language as an aid and a barrier to involvement in the national system', in J. Rubin and B. Jernudd (eds.) (1971), pp. 21-51.

Kloss, Heinz (1969), *Research Possibilities on Group Bilingualism: A report* (Quebec: International Center for Research on Bilingualism).

Kotey, P. A. (1975), 'The official language controversy: indigenous versus colonial', in R. K. Herbert (ed.) (1975), pp. 18-26.

Kuper, Leo and M. G. Smith (eds.) (1969), *Pluralism in Africa* (Berkeley and Los Angeles: University of California Press).

Ladefoged, Peter, Ruth Glick and Clive Criper (eds.) (1972), *Language in Uganda* (London: OUP).

Lambert, W. E. and G. R. Tucker (1972), *Bilingual Education of Children: The St Lambert Experiment* (Rowley: Newbury House Publishers).

Lestage, André (1982), *Literacy and Illiteracy* (Paris: Unesco).

Lieberson, Stanley (1966), 'Language questions in censuses', in

Stanley Lieberson (ed.) (1966), *Explorations in Sociolinguistics* (The Hague: Mouton), pp. 134-51.

Mackey, William F. (1978), 'The importation of bilingual education models', in J. E. Alatis (ed.) (1978), pp. 1-18.

Mackey, William (1984), 'Mother-tongue education: problems and prospects', *Prospects* 14, 1, pp. 37-50.

Mann, Michael and David Dalby (1987), *A Thesaurus of African Languages* (London: Hans Zell Publishers for the International African Institute).

Mazrui, Ali (1969), 'Pluralism and national integration', in L. Kuper and M. G. Smith (eds.) (1969), pp. 333-49.

Mbunda, Fulgens and David Brown (1980), 'Language teaching in primary schools', in E. C. Polomé and G. Hill (eds.) (1980), pp. 283-305.

McConnell, Grant D. (1977), 'Language treatment and language planning', *Language Planning Newsletter*, 3, 3, pp. 1 and 3-6.

McConnell, Grant D. (1979), 'Constructing language profiles by polity', in William F. Mackey and Jacob Ornstein (eds.) (1979), *Sociolinguistic Studies in Language Contact* (The Hague: Mouton), pp. 23-50.

Mehnert, Wolfgang (1973), 'The language question in the colonial policy of German imperialism', *African Studies*, 1, pp. 383-97.

Mhina, G. A. (1976), *Language Planning in Tanzania: Focus on KiSwahili* (Paris: Unesco).

Mulira, E. M. K. (1951), *The Vernacular in African Education* (London: Longmans, Green and Co).

Neustupný, Jiri (1974), 'Basic types of treatment of language problems', in J. Fishman (ed.) (1974), pp. 37-48.

Nida, Eugene A. and William L. Wonderly (1971), 'Communication roles of languages in multilingual societies', in W. H. Whiteley (ed.) (1971), pp. 57-74.

Nieuwenhuijze, C. A. O. van (1982), *Development Begins at Home* (Oxford: Pergamon Press).

Nigeria Educational Research and Development Council (1988), *A Guide for Creating Metalinguistic Terms for African Languages* (Dakar: Unesco Regional Office for Education in Africa).

Noss, R. B. (1971), 'Politics and language policy in Southeast Asia', *Language Sciences*, Bloomington, Indiana, No. 16, pp. 25-32.

Nwoye, Onuigbo G. (1978), *Language Planning in Nigeria*, Ph.D. Dissertation, Georgetown University.

OAU (1986), 'Language plan of action for Africa', Document CM/1352(XLIV), Addis Ababa: OAU Secretariat.

OAU (1988), 'Background information for the consultative meeting on the formation of a Pan-African linguistic association, 7-9 April 1988'. Document CM/1506 (XLVIII) Annex I, Addis Ababa: OAU Secretariat.

O'Barr, William M. (1976), 'Language use and language policy in Tanzania: an overview', in William O'Barr and Jean O'Barr (eds.)

(1976), *Language and Politics* (The Hague: Mouton), pp. 35-48.

Ohannessian, Sirarpi (1978a), 'The teaching of Zambian languages and the preparation of teachers for language teaching in primary schools', in S. Ohannessian and M. E. Kashoki (eds.) (1978), pp. 292-328.

Ohannessian, Sirarpi (1978b), 'English and Zambian languages in secondary schools', in S. Ohannessian and M. E. Kashoki (eds.) (1978), pp. 355-75.

Ohannessian, Sirarpi and Mubanga E. Kashoki (eds.) (1978), *Language in Zambia* (London: International African Institute).

Ohannessian, Sirarpi, Charles Ferguson and Edgar Polomé (eds.) (1975), *Language Surveys in Developing Nations* (Arlington, VA.: Center for Applied Linguistics).

Okonkwo, C. J. E. (1975), 'A function-oriented model of initial language planning in Sub-Saharan Africa', in R. K. Herbert (ed.) (1975), pp. 37-52.

Olabimtan, Afolabi (ed.) (1982), *African Universities and the Development and Wider Use of African Languages* (Lagos: Published under the sponsorship of Unesco).

Omondi, Lucia (1979), 'Paralinguistics: a survey of non-verbal communication with particular reference to Zambia and Kenya', *Journal of the Language Association of Eastern Nigeria*, 4, 1, pp. 19-41.

Opubor, Alfred E. (1973), 'Mass communications in Nigeria', in Ukandi G. Damachi and Hans Dieter Seibel (eds.) (1973), *Social Change and Economic Developments in Nigeria* (New York: Praeger Publishers), pp. 235-52.

Orata, Pedro T. (1953), 'The Iloilo experiment in education through the vernacular', in Unesco (1953), pp. 123-31.

Paden, J. N. (1968), 'Language problems of national integration in Nigeria: the special position of Hausa', in Fishman, Ferguson and Das Gupta (eds.), pp. 199-213.

Pattanayak, Debi P. (1981), *Multilingualism and Mother-tongue Education* (Delhi: OUP).

Polomé, Edgar C. (1975), 'Problems and techniques of a socio-linguistically-oriented language survey: The case of the Tanzania survey', in S. Ohannessian, C. Ferguson and E. C. Polomé (eds.) (1975), pp. 31-50.

Polomé, Edgar C. and C. P. Hill (eds.) (1980), *Language in Tanzania* (Oxford: OUP for the International African Institute).

Pool, Jonathan (1972), 'National development and language diversity', in Joshua A. Fishman (ed.) (1972), *Advances in the Sociology of Language*, pp. 213-30.

Prator, Clifford H. (1972), 'Introduction' in Ladefoged, R. Glick and C. Criper (eds.) (1972), pp. 1-15.

Prator, Clifford H. (1975), 'The survey of language use and language teaching in Eastern Africa in retrospect', in S. Ohannessian, C. Ferguson and E. C. Polomé (eds.) (1975), pp. 145-58.

Rao, Y. V. Lakshmana (1966), *Communication and Development* (Minneapolis: University of Minnesota Press).

Raymaekers, Erik and Myriam Bacquelaine (1985), 'Basic education for rural development', *Prospects* XV, 3, pp. 455-70.

Rice, F. A. (ed.) (1962), *Study of the Role of Second Languages* (Washington, DC: Center for Applied Linguistics).

Rittel, Horst W. J. and Melvin M. Webber (1973), 'Dilemmas in a general theory of planning', *Policy Sciences*, 4, pp. 155-69.

Ross, Jeffrey A. (1979), 'Language and the mobilization of ethnic identity', in H. Giles and B. Saint-Jacques (eds.) (1979), pp. 1-13.

Rubagumya, Casmir M. (1986), 'Language planning in the Tanzanian educational system: problems and prospects', *Journal of Multilingual and Multicultural Development*, 7, 6, pp. 283-300.

Rubin, Joan (1971), 'Evaluation and language planning', in J. Rubin and B. Jernudd (eds.) (1971), pp. 217-52.

Rubin, Joan (1973), 'Language planning: discussion of some current issues', in J. Rubin and R. Shuy (eds.) (1973), pp. 1-10.

Rubin, Joan and Björn Jernudd (eds.) (1971), *Can Language Be Planned?* (Honolulu: The University Press of Hawaii).

Rubin, Joan and Roger Shuy (eds.) (1973), *Language Planning: Current issues and research* (Washington: Georgetown University Press).

Safa, Helen Icken (1974), 'Ethnicity and nation-building: a commentary', in W. Bell and W. E. Freeman (eds.) (1974), pp. 375-77.

Schramm, Wilbur (1964), *Mass Media and National Development* (Stanford: Stanford University Press and Paris: Unesco).

Schumacher, E. F. (1973), *Small is Beautiful* (London: Blond and Briggs Ltd).

Schwarz Jr., F. A. O. (1965), *Nigeria: The tribes, the nation or the race – the politics of independence* (Cambridge, Mass.: MIT Press).

Scotton, Carol (1975), 'Multilingualism in Lagos – what it means to the social scientist', in R. K. Herbert (ed.) (1975), pp. 78-90.

Sebeok, Thomas A. (ed.) (1971), *Linguistics in Sub-Saharan Africa*, Current Trends in Linguistics, Vol. 7 (The Hague: Mouton).

Sengova, Joko (1987), 'The national language of Sierra Leone: a decade of policy experimentation', *Africa*, vol. 57, no. 4, pp. 519-30.

Siguán, Miguel and William F. Mackey (1987), *Education and Bilingualism* (London: Kegan Paul Ltd. in association with Unesco).

Smock, David R. (1975), 'Language policy in Ghana', in Smock and Bentsi-Enchill (eds.) (1975), pp. 169-88.

Smock, David R. and Kwamena Bentsi-Enchill (eds.) (1975), *The Search for National Integration in Africa* (New York: The Free Press).

Soyinka, Wọle (1977), 'The scholar in African society', in A. U. Iwara and E. Mveng (eds.) (1977), *Second World Black and African*

Festival of Arts and Culture: Colloquium on black civilization and education, Vol. 1 (Lagos: Federal Military Government of Nigeria), pp. 44-53.

Spencer, John (ed.) (1963), *Language in Africa* (Cambridge: CUP).

Spencer, John (1971), 'Colonial language policies and their legacies', in Thomas A. Sebeok (ed.) (1971), pp. 537-47.

Spolsky, Bernard (1978), *Educational Linguistics* (Rowley, Mass.: Newbury Publishers).

Srivastava, R. N. (1984), 'Consequences of initiating literacy in the second language', in F. Coulmas (ed.) (1984), pp. 29-37.

Stewart, William A. (1968), 'A sociolinguistic typology for describing national multilingualism', in Joshua A. Fishman (ed.) (1968), *Readings in the Sociology of Language* (The Hague: Mouton), pp. 531-45.

Swain, Merrill (1978), 'Bilingual education for the English-speaking Canadian', in J. E. Alatis (ed.) (1978), pp. 141-54.

Szépe, György (1984), 'Mother tongue, language policy and education', *Prospects*, XIV, 1, pp. 63-73.

Tadadjeu, Maurice (1980), *A Model for Functional Trilingual Education Planning in Africa* (Paris: Unesco).

Tadadjeu, Maurice, G. Gfeller and M. Mba (1985), 'Introducing an official language into an initial mother-tongue education program: the case of Cameroon', Paper presented at the 16th West African Languages Congress, Yaoundé, Cameroon, 25-9 March 1985 (mimeo).

Thompson, Leonard (1969), 'Historical perspectives of pluralism in Africa', in L. Kuper and M. G. Smith (eds.) (1969), pp. 351-71.

Tiffen, Brian (1968), 'Language and education in commonwealth Africa', in J. Dakin, B. Tiffen and H. Widdowson (eds.) (1968), pp. 63-113.

Tollefson, James W. (1981), 'Centralized and decentralized language planning', *Language Problems and Language Planning*, 5, 2, pp. 175-88.

Unesco (1953), *The Use of Vernacular Languages in Education* (Paris: Unesco).

Unesco (1966), *Final Report, Meeting of a Group of Experts for the Unification of Alphabets of National Languages*, Bamako, Mali, 28 February-5 March 1966 (Paris: Unesco).

Unesco (1970), *Functional Literacy* (Paris: Unesco).

Unesco (1972), *Literacy 1969-1971* (Paris: Unesco).

Unesco (1975), *World Communications* (Paris: Unesco).

Unesco (1976a), 'Literacy in the world since the 1965 Teheran Conference: shortcomings, achievements, tendencies', in Leon Bataille (ed.) (1976), pp. 3-33.

Unesco (1976b), 'Experimental world literacy programme report and synthesis of evaluation', in Leon Bataille (ed.) (1976), pp. 35-62.

Unesco (1977), *Education in Africa in the Light of the Lagos Conference* (Paris: Unesco).

Unesco (1979), *Meeting of Experts on the Use of Regional or Sub-regional African Languages as Media of Culture and Communication within the Continent.* Bamako, Mali, 18-22 June 1979 (Paris: Unesco).

Unesco (1981a), *Bibliography of Major Decisions, Meetings and Documents Related to Unesco's Activities in the Domain of Mother Tongue Instruction and Languages* (Paris: Unesco).

Unesco (1981b), *African Languages* (Proceedings of the Meeting of Experts on the transcription and harmonization of African languages, Niamey (Niger), 17-21 July 1978) (Paris: Unesco).

Unesco (1987), *Statistical Yearbook* (Paris: Unesco).

Ure, Jean (1981), 'Mother tongue education and minority languages: a question of values and costs', *Journal of Multilingual and Multicultural Development*, 2, 4, pp. 303-8.

Van den Berge, Pierre L. (1969), 'Pluralism and the polity: a theoretical exploration', in L. Kuper and M. G. Smith (eds.) (1969), pp. 67-81.

Walusimbi, Livingstone (1972), 'Language in education', in Peter Ladefoged, Ruth Glick and Clive Criper (eds.) (1972), pp. 85-142.

Weiner, Myron (1967), 'A note on communication and development in India', in Daniel Lerner and Wilbur Schramm (eds.) (1967), *Communication and Change in the Developing Countries* (Honolulu: East West Center Press), pp. 190-4.

Weinstein, Brian (1980), 'Language planning in francophone Africa', *Language Problems and Language Planning*, 4, 1, pp. 55-77.

Weinstein, Brian (1983), *The Civic Tongue: Political consequences of language choice* (New York: Longman Inc).

West Africa, 23 May 1988.

White, John (1980), 'The historical background to national education in Tanzania', in E. Polomé and C. Hill (eds.) (1980), pp. 261-82.

Whiteley, W. H. (1968), 'Ideal and reality in national language policy', in J. Fishman, C. Ferguson and J. Das Gupta (eds.) (1968), pp. 327-44.

Whiteley, W. H. (ed.) (1971), *Language Use and Social Change* (London: OUP for the International African Institute).

Whiteley, W. H. (ed.) (1974), *Language in Kenya* (Nairobi: OUP).

Williams, Glyn (1986), 'Language planning or language expropriation?', *Journal of Multilingual and Multicultural Development*, 7, 6, pp. 509-18.

Williamson, Kay (1976a), 'The Rivers Readers Project in Nigeria', in Bamgboṣe (ed.) (1976), pp. 135-53.

Williamson, Kay (1976b), *Practical Orthography* (Ibadan: Heinemann Educational Books (Nig.) Ltd).

Williamson, Kay (1979), 'Small languages in primary education: The Rivers Readers Project as a case history', *African Languages*, 5, 2, pp. 95-105.

Williamson, Kay (ed.) (1985), *West African Languages in Education* (Wien: Veröffentlichungen der Institut für Afrikanistik und

Ägyptologie der Universität Wien).

Wolff, Hans (1954), *Nigerian Orthography* (Zaria: Gaskiya Corporation).

Wolff, Hans (1964), 'Intelligibility and inter-ethnic attitudes', in Dell Hymes (ed.) (1964), pp. 440-5.

Index